THE WELFARE CITY IN TRANSITION – A COMPILATION OF TEXTS AND IMAGES 1923–2020

Contents

URGENCY

INTRODUCTION
IN SEARCH OF THE WELFARE CITY

The welfare city as we know it is facing structural challenges that undermine the ideology known from early welfarism. We have already passed the turning point where the welfare city entered a new phase of market-driven development, changing the demographic profile of our cities. Emerging out of the ashes of war, ruins and fascism after the end of WWII, the post-war welfare city and its architects faced many of the same crises we are facing today: financial crisis, migration crisis, democracy crisis, housing crisis, health crisis etc. How can we learn from the experiences of the past to better tackle the challenges of the present and the future? In addition, the major 'newcomer' crisis of climate change has proved that clean air, drinking water and green spaces are no longer just resources for progress and growth but common amenities in need of care with a 'post-human' era approaching fast. How can architecture and urban planning thus support the ambition of Copenhagen to become carbon-neutral in 2025, and Denmark in 2050, while securing welfare, equality and health – not only for humans but for other species and the environment as well?

Furthermore, Danish cities such as Copenhagen and Aarhus are transforming from inclusive and egalitarian welfare cities to 'wealth cities' for the well-off as the welfare concept gradually loses its function as the primary urban policy indicator. The post-war welfare city's planning ideals of transparency, accessibility and openness, echoing the social programmes of the welfare state, are contrasted by the invariable logic of the competition-based and market-driven wealth city, which is increasingly gaining ground. As it is, this shift from the notion of a good life from cradle to grave for the many towards a branding-based liveability calls for an examination of the legacy of the welfare city and of the values underpinning the future development of our cities.

The post-war welfare city was primarily planned and managed by the state and the municipality. However, since the neoliberal turn a globalized economy and interurban competition have been affecting the city's local development and the housing and real estate market. More stakeholders and private interests are involved in the urban development and construction of new urban neighbourhoods and housing units.

The modernist welfare city has recently gained new significance as a majority in the Danish parliament passed the 'Ghetto Package', vowing to transform post-war social housing estates, designated as 'ghettos', through demolitions, densification, new housing typologies and displacement of 'disadvantaged' residents. Yet, is it possible to create a socially balanced city while maintaining the egalitarian qualities of social housing (Danish: *almen bolig*), including its value as cultural heritage? Are we creating new tabula rasa plans, or are we able to learn from the failures of modernism?

The theme of this year's Copenhagen Architecture Festival is 'The Welfare City in Transition' – a focus that continues our ongoing examination of the welfare city and its transformations, e.g. in the form of a branch of the architecture festival in Tingbjerg in 2016, the Lacaton & Vassal exhibition 'Never Demolish!' in Gellerup Museum in 2017, an open film competition on social housing estates in 2018, the publication *MANIFEST STAFET*, which presented 49 manifestos on the role of architecture in society in 2019, and in 2020 a compilation of open letters to Copenhagen's Lord Mayor, Frank Jensen, giving advice on how to reach the city's ambitious goal of carbon-neutrality in 2025.

During the process of editing this book, the force majeure of Covid-19 took centre stage, influencing cities and society in unprecedented ways and highlighting the relevance of studying the welfare city in transition. Welfare city issues such as management of public space, (in)equality, health and hygiene in relation to architecture, biopolitics, infrastructure and mobility, home and work balances, the role of care in public institutions, recreation and tourism etc. reappeared in new contexts as the Danish Prime Minister, Mette Frederiksen, imposed a lockdown on society on 11 March 2020. How the pandemic will affect urban life in the long run, let alone possibly stimulate a green transition within architecture and urbanism, is yet too early to predict. So far, Covid-19 has underlined that inequality still exists and that housing patterns and priorities of urban planning are affecting contamination rates in major ways. Thus, both are key factors to be analysed while developing containment strategies. Furthermore, the pandemic has proved that it can be challenging to take care of the health and welfare of local citizens while maintaining the economic connectivities of tourism, international sports and entertainment events. Covid-19 has shown the value and robustness of having a strong welfare state with its public welfare institutions, regulations and top-down planning. Thus, it gives momentum to reconsider our values.

READING INSTRUCTIONS

This publication is a carefully selected compilation of themes and statements that (re)examine the welfare city of the past and the present in order to address issues of the future. The aim is not to define what the welfare city is in a static way. Rather, through the dynamics of juxtaposing excerpts of texts and images from different sources, the composite material creates a map as a basis for discussing, negotiating and acting in the ambivalent context of the welfare city.

As a hybrid, heterogeneous volume, made with an attitude of experiment from our side, the book reflects the complexity of the subject. Therefore, we have created a contextualization and a framework via introducing chapters and captions to guide the readers. We have compiled text excerpts and images from newspapers, architectural journals, fiction, snapshots, renderings, posters, plans, artworks, interviews, graffiti, statistics, academic papers etc. The book can be read from A to Z, or you can browse through it and make your own connections and comparisons along the way.

Geographically, the focus is on Denmark – especially Copenhagen with the Finger Plan suburbs and partly Aarhus. Yet, we have included international sources where it seemed relevant to add new perspectives to the Danish context – not least in the third chapter, which covers a period where the world is increasingly more connected. With all their aspirations, hopes and fears, these texts and images portray the hard-fought urbanistic battle of early welfarism, the critique of it, and current transitions. We are well aware that a selection of texts will just be glimpses of the larger picture, but taken together the quotes and images summarize some of the most important positions in Danish urbanism over the past 75-80 years. Through three chapters – 'Critique and Utopia' focusing on the past, 'Status' concentrating on the present, and 'Urgency' outlining future perspectives and challenges – the book portrays different aspects of the development of the welfare state, with the heartfelt hope that the welfare city will prove to be more than just a thing of the past.

Copenhagen, August 2020

1.

Critique and Utopia

The welfare planning regime was rooted in a firm belief in modernity and progress. The progressive utopian framework created by the European and American modernist avant-garde movements like the Bauhaus played an important role in the urban imaginary of early welfare architecture and city planning. In short, rational principles based on ideals originating from the Enlightenment would lead to the construction of high-end planning and housing schemes across the Western world and would eventually be exported to other continents. Standing on the broad shoulders of the social movements of the time, the utopian dream of liberating the masses – primarily the new working class of rural-urban migrants attracted by the rising industries of growing cities – through architecture and urban planning seemed like a plausible scenario. The moralism associated with the modern movement was unsentimental and infused with the post-war era's aesthetic thinking and endless energy and faith in growth and progress. After World War II, where housing shortage and a momentum for a new beginning in the industrializing and urbanizing welfare state were prevalent, the need for urban planning had never been more pressing. The omnipotent discipline of city planning as a liberating driver for social change, happiness and modernization became the prism through which the thinking and doing of a generation of urbanists such as Le Corbusier, Ernst May, Hannes Meyer and their international peers of the CIAM (Congrès Internationaux d'Architecture Moderne) and later Team X manifested themselves most clearly.

According to the ideological planners, all the aspirations of utopian thinking could finally be turned into concrete reality. Politically and ideologically, this happened in parallel to the full implementation of the welfare state model and the regulation of the citizens' life from cradle to grave with social engineering. In a Danish context, social engineering became a way of promoting the primarily Social Democratic egalitarian values and the hope that it would be possible to improve the lives of the many in just one generation. Hence, housing policy was – and is – an ideological stronghold of the welfare state as a prime instrument to lift people out of poverty and slum and upgrading their lifestyles to modern standards.

Planning created the physical framework of the welfare state and incarnated its ideology of egalitarianism, progress and community. Thus, urban planners and architects worked closely with politicians of the state and the municipality to form the ideal framework of everyday life in the welfare city. The rest is history. Or so it would seem. A few decades later, criticism of the megalomaniac drive associated with the modernist master plans took hold. During 'the glorious 30 years' of 1945-1975, the building effort was massive and efficient. Certain critics argued that quantity trumped quality in some of the biggest housing estates, and New Towns as social engineering and bureaucracy took the lead, while artistic innovation and poetry were neglected. After the minimum standards and basic needs were covered, new questions about the quality of life and space for difference/diversity arose. Among the most prominent critics were the Situationists, the American journalist Jane Jacobs, the Danish architect Jan Gehl and urban activists in the wake of 1968. The critique continued in later clashes between top-down planning efforts and bottom-up initiatives of local residents. The argument that the mega plans would eventually overwrite the values of traditional placemaking, historical identity, local building heritage and ultimately freedom of expression of the individual was thus a strong counter argument to the universal ideas of modernist planning. The grid versus organic urban growth. The universal versus the particular. A criticism that still lives on today.

Thus, during the past three decades, the welfare city and the welfare society have experienced massive changes economically, demographically and culturally. Copenhagen is an illustrative case to examine urban transformations and tendencies which extend beyond the national borders as city centres are gaining global importance as attractors for capital and culture. During the late 1980s, Copenhagen was one of the poorest municipalities in Denmark with a run-down stock of housing and a population of less affluent taxpayers and welfare recipients. Following the 1990s' big urban initiatives, such as the metro, newly built neighbourhoods such as Ørestad and the regeneration of old blue-collar districts such as Nørrebro and Vesterbro, the capital has become one of the richest Danish municipalities, an attractive city for tourists, investors and newcomers to settle in – if they can afford it. This development raises questions of the right to the city, segregation within the municipal borders and the level of in/exclusion of particular groups.

ARCHITECTURE IN THE WELFARE STATE

An area that currently sees an upsurge in interest is the under-described relationship between the political and social aspects of the post-war welfare state, on the one hand, and the architecture and urbanism of the period 1945–1975, on the other. The publication of the anthology *Architecture and the Welfare State* (2015), edited by the international trio of architectural historians and researchers Mark Swenarton, Tom Avermaete and Dirk van Heuvel, is one of the most comprehensive attempts to map both the social, political and material aspects of the welfare state in an international perspective.

> 'In the decades following the Second World War, and partly in response to the Cold War, governments across Western Europe set out ambitious programmes for social welfare and the redistribution of wealth that aimed to improve the everyday lives of their citizens. Many of these welfare state programmes – housing, schools, New Towns, cultural and leisure centres – involved not just construction but a new approach to architectural design in which the welfare objectives of these state-funded programmes were delineated and debated. The impact on architects and architectural design was profound and far-reaching, with welfare state projects moving centre-stage in architectural discourse, not just in Europe but worldwide (...) the planning of the built environment – from New Towns, to social housing, to schools and universities, hospitals and health centres, to leisure and sports complexes, to arts centres – was one of the key areas in which the welfare state sought to achieve its ambitions of economic redistribution and social welfare.'

(Mark Swenarton, Tom Avermaete and Dirk van den Heuvel (eds.), *Architecture and the Welfare State*, Abingdon/NewYork: Routledge, 2015, pp. 0-2)

HAPPY: CITIES AND PUBLIC HAPPINESS IN POST-WAR EUROPE

An earlier example of an anthology that examines post-war architecture and urbanism in different cultural and political contexts on both sides of the Iron Curtain is *Happy: Cities and Public Happiness in Post-War Europe* (2004), edited by Cor Wagenaar, who is a professor of the History and Theory of Architecture and Urbanism at TU Delft. It is fascinating to compare different regions, pointing out similarities and differences between countries across the Nordic welfare states, the communist Eastern Block and Western Europe. Despite their differences, they all used planning to create the ideal city of the future according to a utopian vision of 'the good life' and happiness for 'the people'.

'Sometimes, architecture and town planning are used to promote public happiness. There is no shortage of bright, attractive, and also tricky and subversive imagery presenting yesterday's vision of tomorrow's cities as places where everybody will be happy ... [T]he transformation of the European city after 1945 has been guided by this type of imagery. The urban landscape reflects specific ideals about happiness. Not, however, of the private happiness one may experience in the intimacy of one's home, but of public happiness ... If happiness becomes a public affair, the public domain is the setting where town planners stage their icons, and all these icons carry promises of happiness. Who defines these promises? Obviously, the clients: politicians, developers, marketing experts. Does that corrupt these icons? If so, does it diminish their appeal?'

(Kristin Feiress in Cor Wagenaar (ed.), *Happy: Cities and Public Happiness in Post-War Europe*, Rotterdam: NAi Publishers, 2004, p. 9)

'THE WELFARE CITY CONCEPT'

In the early 2000s, the Aarhus School of Architecture embarked on a major research project about architecture and the welfare state. One of the outcomes was a special issue of the journal *Nordisk Arkitekturforskning* (*the Nordic Journal of Architectural Research*), in which the sociologist Niels Albertsen and the sociologist and architect Bülent Diken tried to formulate a concept of the welfare city.

'On this background a concept of "the welfare city" seems meaningful. On the one hand the ideas of architecture and urban planning, which shaped urban development in the years after the Second World War, were closely linked to the utilitarian ideas that are a founding part of welfare thinking in general. On the other hand this urban development, like the welfare state, was highly influenced by state interventionism. The utilitarian ideas were codified into the CIAM charter, which also gathered "the principles and ways of thinking from Taylorism, Fordism, and in a certain way Keynesianism and the welfare state" (Ascher 2002: 30). These principles became so influential after the Second World War that the urban development of these years has been characterized as a "taylo-fordo-keynésio-corbusian" period (Ascher 1995: 86). It must, however, be expected that the concept of the welfare city is just as heterogeneous, ambivalent and contested as the concepts of welfare, the welfare state or welfare regimes. In so far as the concept of the welfare city refers to urban built environments and urban ways of living, which have developed under the influence of the welfare state, this influence must be expected to vary according to the different forms of welfare regimes.'

(N. Albertsen & B. Diken, 'Welfare and the City'. *Nordisk Arkitekturforskning*, vol. 17 (2) 2004, pp. 7-22)

THE RISE OF THE DANISH WELFARE STATE

Published in 2017, the anthology *Forming Welfare* gathered contributions from many prominent researchers to examine links between architecture and the welfare state in a Danish context, including the myths of the humanist welfare architect working for the common good (rather than for private developers and more commercial interests), and a rare convergence between the architectural model of the welfare city and the political model of the welfare state with their social visions. Below is an excerpt of the introduction by Katrine Lotz, an associate professor at KADK in Copenhagen.

'First of all, it is important to distinguish between a number of terms. "Welfare" is a generic and rather vague term that covers both concrete help to those that need it and notions of "a good life" for the individual or the community. "Welfare society" is an idealized notion of the good society that allows every one of its citizens to realize his/her full potential in safety, freedom, relative prosperity and – according to the common understanding also – political freedom. The term 'welfare state' is introduced in the 1950s, first as a political and then an analytical concept, primarily applied to the fields of economy, political science and sociology, which focuses on concrete and long-established balances between the state, the civil society and the market, and various modes of economic regulation.

The many town hall extensions and annexes that were built in the 1930s were a direct result of the new and comprehensive social legislation. They provided the space that was needed for new kinds of employees and new kinds of meetings between citizen and municipality. This is a good example of the direct impact that legislation has had on the built environment. Another example is the development of new school building typologies, which has often happened as a natural consequence of new legislation within the field. A recent case in point is Ørestad High School, where class space and shared space are two among a number of elements within a large hall that spans the entire height and length of the building. The direct cause of this typological innovation was the passing of a new high school reform. The same causal relationship applies to the construction of kindergartens, universities, hospitals, nursing homes, prisons, mental hospitals and, not least, culture facilities where architecture has been, and still is, a determining factor when it comes to orchestrating the citizen's meeting with the State. The extensive evolution of the public institutions can, in many ways, be seen as the most obvious spatial and material manifestation of the burgeoning welfare state and its basic values.'

(Katrine Lotz, 'Introduction', *Forming Welfare*, Copenhagen: The Danish Architectural Press, 2017, 1st edition)

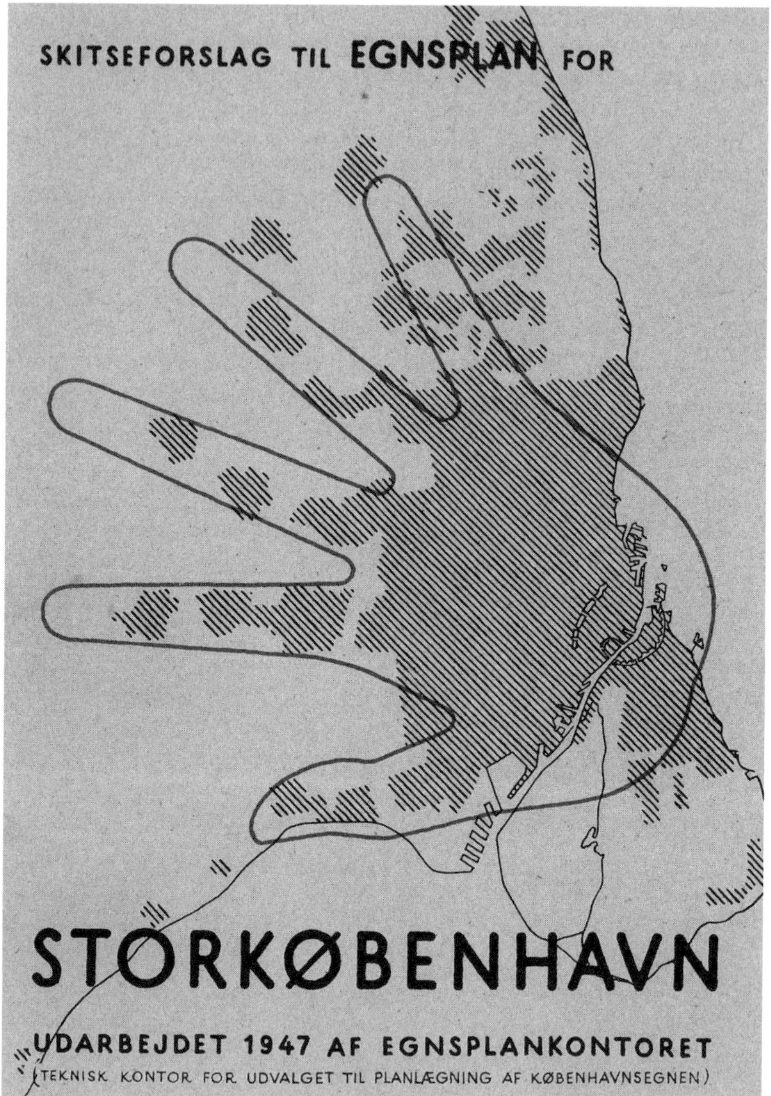

The Finger Plan of 1947 by Egnsplankontoret. (Courtesy of Dansk Byplanlaboratorium)

In 2008, Professor at the Aarhus School of Architecture Tom Nielsen wrote a history of urbanism from the post-war period until the beginning of the 21st century with its changing ideals and political paradigm shifts. Here, he writes about some of the founding pillars of Danish welfare urbanism, including Copenhagen's regional Finger Plan and the Ministry of Housing, both established in 1947.

'The notion of a state-run, planned welfare Denmark resulted in a large planning apparatus as part of the large public service sector, which, with the Keynesian economic policy, was established in the post-war years. This development took place from the very beginning of the establishment of the Ministry of Housing and Construction in 1947 under the Social Democratic government, and by extension the adoption of the City Regulation Act of 1949 (...) Thus, the most important thing about the law was that construction in agricultural areas would also require permission, and that it paved the way for the creation of committees to coordinate new urban growth, so that it could reasonably take place across municipal boundaries. This was the beginning of a more regional view of urban planning than what had previously been practised. Here, an important source of inspiration was the "Sketch Proposal for a Regional Plan for Greater Copenhagen" (known as the "Finger Plan"), which was presented in 1947.'

(Tom Nielsen, *Gode Intentioner og uregerlige byer.* Aarhus: Arkitektskolens Forlag, 2008, pp. 58-59)

HAND IN GLOVE – COPENHAGEN'S FINGER PLAN

Inspired by Patrick Abercrombie's seminal Greater London Plan that was smuggled into Denmark via Swedish boats during WWII, the work on Copenhagen's Finger Plan began in March 1945. Steen Eiler Rasmussen and Peter Bredsdorff, the two leading architects, conceptualized the new regional plan as a glove fitting metropolitan Copenhagen's expansion along five new 'fingers'; each finger consisting of a railway line along which suburbs and New Towns could grow, separated by green wedges. Cities around the world, from Stockholm to Singapore, were later inspired by the Finger Plan. Launched in 1947, the plan has guided the Danish capital's development and has been updated several times, although never officially legalized as the regional plan.

INTRODUCTION BY CHAIRMAN OF THE REGIONAL PLANNING COMMITTEE, PROFESSOR STEEN EILER RASMUSSEN

'An overall plan for the development of an entire metropolitan area must of course become a very complicated task, just as the metropolitan society itself is complicated. All relationships are interrelated, interwoven. One cannot plan one part of the city without considering the planning of the other districts. And one cannot plan the traffic lines rationally without simultaneously planning the buildings that generate the traffic, not plan housing areas without simultaneously thinking of business areas and outdoor areas for the new residents, etc.

In order to formulate a comprehensive plan for all these conditions, one must examine them on the basis of an overall presumption of the future size of the population, business distribution, space requirements, etc. Only when you have such a hypothesis as a point of departure can you come up with a plan where everything fits (...) Only time will tell to what extent the thoughts that one can have today about the future development will come true.'

(Egnsplankontoret, 'Skitseforslag til egnsplan for Storkøbenhavn'. Copenhagen: Egnsplankonteret, 1947. Reprinted by Dansk Byplanlaboratorium in 1993, pp. 9-10)

MAN AND MASTER PLAN: THE ARCHITECT AS ARTIST AND SOCIAL ENGINEER

Asger Jorn was a Danish artist and founding member of the international avant-garde groups CoBrA and Situationist International. Throughout his long career, Jorn was interested in architecture and not least the Swiss architect Le Corbusier for whom he worked during the world exhibition in Paris in 1937. Jorn was at once fascinated and disgusted by the great modernist's grand visions of architecture and urbanism. These excerpts of the article in *Arkitekten* from 1947 are based on a lecture he gave in 1946 in the Jutland branch of the Danish Association of Architects, where he proclaimed the failure of Modernism based on Le Corbusier's book *The Home of Man* (1945). Later, Jorn developed his critique of the (over)rational modernist master plan in Situationist International with Guy Debord a.o., stressing the importance of everyday life, subjectivity and the right to the city.

'In order to liberate architecture from the extinct idiom of craftsmanship, to set free the possibilities of the new epoch, of the machine, of industrialism it was necessary to mobilize a formalism that was so negative, so life defying, inhibitory and academically traditional as one can possibly imagine.

Today, we are facing the task of liberating ourselves from the foundation of fake and negative assertions that were used as a necessary midwifery for the new era's architecture in the period of modernism and contructivism. Modernism is the architecture of industrialism. It is therefore the architecture of both private capitalism and democracy.

(...)

'What are the aesthetics of Le Corbusier? A belief in the beauty of his rationalism, his worship of reason. Rather than worshipping life, Le Corbusier worships reason, logic. What is not reasonable is neglected and annulled (...) Modernism is constructed without desire, i.e. for dead people.'

(Asger Jorn, 'Menneskeboliger eller Tankekonstruktioner i Jernbeton', *Arkitekten Ugehæfte* 16-17, 1947, pp. 61-68)

Le Corbusier is one of the most well-known and important modernist architects and urban planners. His ideas of 'living machines' and the rational mega cities of 'la ville radieuse' were highly influential and later re-appeared in second and third generation social housing estates of varying quality. He was a founding member of the Congrès Internationaux d'Architecture Moderne (CIAM), and retrospectively explained that his modernist housing designs were intended as places for meditation and contemplation. In 2016, 17 of his constructions across the world were included on UNESCO's list of World Heritage.

'The Plan is the generator.

Without a plan, you have lack of order, and wilfulness.

The plan holds in itself the essence of sensation.

The great problems of to-morrow, dictated by collective necessities, put the question of 'plan' in a new form.

Modern life demands, and is waiting for, a new kind of plan
both for the house and the city.'

(Le Corbusier: *Towards a New Architecture.* New York: Dover Publications, 1923/1986, p. 45)

Housing conditions in the old part of Copenhagen were often poor and overcrowded. Following the tradition of an older Danish photographer, Jacob A. Riis and his photographs of slum in New York, Bror Bernild published the book *Can we tolerate this?* (*Kan vi være det bekendt?*) in 1946, documenting slum-like living conditions in Copenhagen. Criticizing the welfare city with its utilitarian mass housing and rational master plans, we tend to forget this recent past when a workers' family, moving from a cramped flat on Nørrebro, was able to upgrade their dwelling to a modernist 'paradise' with bathroom, kitchen and daylight in one of the new neighbourhoods. (Kjeld de Fine Licht/KADK DOCS)

Denmark's first residential high-rise development, the Bellahøj Houses, located picturesquely in an organic landscape on one of Copenhagen's topographically highest plots, was a seminal project based on a competition that redefined housing in the post-war period. Looking at Tingbjerg and Bellahøj, we can see an ongoing discussion between principles of a Le Corbusier-like plan of high-rises in a park, and an English garden city-like approach with lower blocks and neighbourhood planning. The competition took place already during WWII, featuring many well-known architects such as Svenn Eske Kristensen and Edvard Heiberg, who designed the communal house that included a restaurant and other common facilities. The landscape architect C. Th. Sørensen, who designed the wide range of organic open spaces including the iconic amphitheatre, ended up living in the Bellahøj houses himself. Some of the unrealized projects of the competition were quite radical – including the proposition of a 48-storey high-rise development that would have dominated Copenhagen's skyline completely. The new construction methods of the Bellahøj houses reinvented Danish housing design with their use of prefabricated building elements. Initially, the Bellahøj houses were nicknamed 'the Oatmeal Houses' since the rent was very expensive in spite of it being social housing, and therefore it was mused that the residents would have to eat oatmeal to be able to afford living there.

> 'I believe you can say that all possibilities for construction in the area have been thoroughly examined and that the result demonstrates the significance it has, when there is reasonable possibility therefore, to hold a competition, not only to thereby have all possibilities exhaustingly examined, but also because for architects it is of great value to be given the opportunity to work on alternate projects and present new viewpoints. However, the competition also demonstrates that amongst architects there is a very strong interest in the free-standing high-rise block, just as one senses a clear tendency towards the separated and differentiated structure in the majority of the submitted projects as opposed to the large, closed but also rather coarse construction elements that were used previously.
>
> We, who are working with housing on a daily basis and practically every day see with frustration the types of flats that are both too small and too poorly equipped, cannot but be surprised by the disproportion there is between the abundant resources being spent on the construction of schools, hospitals and other public constructions, let alone factories, and the resources appointed to housing. After all, it is in the home that we human beings spend the majority of our

time, and yet the flats are spatially far inferior. Nevertheless, it is not solely a matter of providing better and larger flats. It is equally a matter of ensuring that the areas that surround our houses are formed in such a way that some of the contact with the green, with nature, that we have missed for too many years, is reestablished.'

(Svenn Eske Kristensen, 'Konkurrencen om Bebyggelse paa Bellahøj', *Arkitekten* 47, 1945, p. 19)

THE NEIGHBOURHOOD AND THE CITY PLAN

Edvard Heiberg, a Communist who taught at the Bauhaus school in the beginning of the 1930s and worked for Le Corbusier and at the urban planning office in Soviet Moscow with Ernst May, was one of the pioneers of social housing in Denmark. In his reflections on the situation in Denmark around 1941, you can see how politics, economy and class affected his ideas. In the text below, he is considering the rapid changes that housing design was undergoing in the period just before and during World War II.

'Ten years ago, the common shape of the residential area was the square block with facades towards all four corners of the world. Balconies were a rare luxury even in better standard flats, and amongst architects almost a naughty word. All living rooms were facing the street, regardless of orientation. Bedrooms and kitchens were facing towards a concrete backyard with drying racks and carpet hangers, outdoor loos and garbage bins. When you arrive from these older neighbourhoods to one of the modern park estates such as Ryparken, the development is striking. The orientation of the blocks with west-facing living rooms seems convincing on a summer's afternoon when the balconies with their varied awnings are occupied by residents in the western sun, having returned from work and enjoying the siesta with the radio on full volume and the coffee pot on the table, while the children are tumbling on the green grass beneath the willows in the broad green belts between the houses.

That one here faces a cultural progress achieved over the short time span of merely 10 years, yet of grander significance than what has otherwise happened within housing during the past couple of centuries, will probably be admitted by even the grumpiest of retrogressives.

(...) It must be acknowledged that the municipality of Copenhagen has had a considerable impact on the reduced plot ratio in the new neighbourhoods, in part via the department of city planning, and in part via the magistrate's second department through sales of the municipality's own plots.

(...)

In the development of the large new residential areas one finds a tendency towards an organized small society, which I believe is a progress. It not only ensures a financial benefit that numerous people at once can utilize a large central heating system, washing facilities, playgrounds and park areas, youth clubs and kindergartens, it also develops a sense of community as it was known in the village but lost by the individualistic city dweller who often does not even know the neighbour on the other side of the staircase. (...) The residential area should not merely be a place where one sleeps at night but rather a place where one belongs.'

(Edvard Heiberg, 'Socialt Boligbyggeri', published in 1941 by Foreningen Socialt Boligbyggeri, Copenhagen. Ed. architect Ole Buhl)

The Bellahøj Houses (photos by C. Th. Sørensen/KADK DOCS).

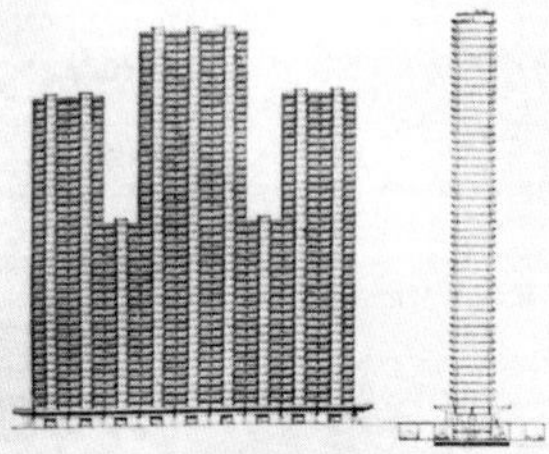

Mogens Krarup i Samarbejde med Civilingeniørerne Steensen og Warming: Bebyggelse paa Bellahøj
Ikke-præmieret Konkurrenceforslag. Snit og Facade 1 : 8000

Projekt nr. 22810 er udarbejdet af civilingeniørerne Steensen og Warming og arkitekt Mogens Krarup og viser, hvorledes man blot ved placeringen af en enkelt blok vil kunne opnaa rimelig udnyttelse af grunden, men det viser rigtignok ogsaa, at den viste bebyggelse i 48 etager helt vil dominere byens silhouet, ligesom den høje bebyggelse vil kaste voldsomme skygger paa det omkringliggende terræn.

Hvilket Resultat kan man uddrage af den afholdte Konkurrence?

Jeg tror man kan sige, at alle muligheder for arealets bebyggelse er blevet grundigt belyst, og resultatet viser, hvor stor betydning det har, at man, naar der er rimelig lejlighed dertil, afholder konkurrencer, ikke alene for derved at faa alle muligheder udtømmende belyst, men ogsaa fordi det er af stor værdi for arkitekter paa denne maade at faa lejlighed til at arbejde med vekslende opgaver og faa fremsat nye synspunkter. Men konkurrencen viser ogsaa, at der blandt arkitekter er en meget stor interesse for det fritliggende høje hus, ligesom man gennem hovedparten af de indsendte projekter mærker en tydelig tendens mod den opdelte og differentierede bygning, i modsætning til de store sluttede, men ogsaa ret grove bygningslegemer man tidligere har arbejdet med.

Vi, der til daglig beskæftiger os med boligbyggeri og praktisk talt hver dag konstaterer egen utilfredshed med de lejlighedstyper, der baade er for smaa og for daarligt udstyrede, kan ikke undgaa at forbavses over det misforhold, der er mellem de rigelige midler, der ofres paa skolebyggeri, hospitalsbyggeri og andet officielt byggeri, ja endog paa fabriksbyggeri, og de midler der ofres paa boligbyggeri. I boligen skal vi mennesker dog tilbringe hovedparten af vor tid, og lejlighederne er langt ringere i rummæssig henseende. Men det er ikke alene et spørgsmaal om at skaffe bedre og større lejligheder. Det er i lige saa høj grad et spørgsmaal om at sørge for, at de arealer som omgiver vore huse udformes paa en saadan maade, at der igen knyttes lidt af den kontakt med det grønne, med naturen, som vi i altfor mange aar har savnet. Vore bestræbelser for at opnaa denne kontakt modvirkes imidlertid i meget høj grad af brandmæssige krav. Naar man betragter den tre-etagers bebyggelse, er det slaaende, at der her kan opnaas intim kontakt mellem det grønne omraade og husene, men saasnart man bygger højere, spiller brandvæsenets krav ind, og husenes nærmeste omgivelser maa forsynes med kørebaner. Naar man derfor betragter resultaterne af denne konkurrence, kan man ikke undgaa at blive bekymret for, at konkurrencens resultat i nogen grad forflygtiges, hvis husenes omgivelser ikke bliver det grønne areal, som er forudset, men derimod golde vejbaner.

Det er mit haab, at det maa lykkes den kommende generation at skabe bebyggelser, som løser problemerne.

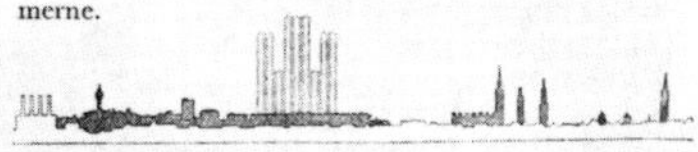

To Værker om Bygningsret

351.785 (489)

Dansk Bygningsret. Af Viggo Vasegaard, cand. jur. og polyt., Ekspeditionssekretær i Københavns Magistrat. G. E. C. Gads Forlag. 432 Sider.

Om Anledningen til dette digre Værks Fremkomst oplyses i Forordet bl. a. følgende: „Efter Ikrafttrædelsen af Byggeloven for Staden København af 29. Marts 1939 den 1. Januar 1940 er den tidligere af Landsdommer A. Gøtzsche udgivne Fremstilling af den danske Bygningsret – der iøvrigt i længere Tid har været udsolgt, hvilket ogsaa er Tilfældet med Kontorchef E. Sivertsens kommenterede Udgave af Byggeloven for København – blevet forældet, hvorfor en ny Fremstilling af denne Disciplin nu er paakrævet. Landsdommer Gøtzsches Bog havde, som det ogsaa fremgaar af Forordet, hovedsagelig til Formaal at danne Grundlag for Undervisningen paa Kunstakademiets bygningstekniske Skole og Det tekniske Selskabs Skole i København, men ved Udarbejdelsen af en ny Fremstilling af dansk Bygningsret har jeg imidlertid ikke ment at burde have et saa begrænset Formaal for Øje, idet jeg har Erfaring for, at der ogsaa uden for de studerendes Kreds, blandt Arkitekter, Ingeniører, Sagførere, Ejendomsmæglere, administrative og judicielle Embedsmænd m. fl. er et praktisk Behov for Kendskab til de efterhaanden mere og mere komplicerede Regler, der retligt normerer Bygningernes Placering, Opførelse, Indretning og Benyttelse.“ Og endvidere oplyses i Forordet: „Af Hensyn til de Studerende er de Dele af Fremstillingen, der ligger uden for, hvad disse bør have Kendskab til, sat med petite. Skønnes yderligere Begrænsning af Stoffet til Undervisningen paakrævet, maa denne foretages af vedkommende Lærer.“

A. Gøtzsches Bygningsret var skrevet fortrinsvis som Lærebog for Undervisning af Elever ved de tekniske Læreanstalter. Men derfor kunde den meget vel ogsaa være til Nytte for Arkitekter, Jurister, Bygnings-

19

The futuristic 48-storey superblock proposed by architect Mogens Krarup and civil engineers Steensen and Warming. The entry was not among the prizewinners of the Bellahøj competition. Competition proposal: sectional view and facade: 1:8000. (Svenn Eske Kristensen, 'Konkurrencen om Bebyggelse paa Bellahøj', Arkitekten 47, 1945, p. 10)

‘Children playing on the grass in Ryparken’. (From the book *Socialt Boligbyggeri*, 1941, Copenhagen: Foreningen af Socialt Boligbyggeri)

German refugees in Kløvermarken: from 1945 until 1949, barracks located on Kløvermarken on Amager temporarily accommodated around 18,000 of the approximately 240,000 German refugees which had been displaced from eastern parts of the Third Reich after the 'liberation' by the Red Army. Supplied by the Swedish wood industry, the barracks occupied 2,200 Danish workers in October 1945 (while Danish Jewish refugees returned from Sweden). Initially, the intention was to place the camp on the animal fair ground of Bellahøjmarken, but that plan was abandoned after resistance from farmers. In August 1946, 17,798 refugees resided in the Kløvermarken camp. The refugees were contained but strictly segregated from the Danish society – it was against the law for Danes and Germans to communicate. Thus, there was an entire infrastructure of basic facilities and services inside the camp. In total, there were 92,000 German refugees in the Copenhagen area, distributed across 151 camps. Kløvermarken was in operation until 1947, when most of the refugees were sent back to Germany, but a smaller part of the camp continued until February 1949. Many refugees died – not infrequently because of a lack of medical care. Around 5,344 refugees are buried at Vestre Kirkegård (Western Cemetery). (Aerial photo by Sylvest Jensen courtesy of The Royal Library in Copenhagen) (Courtesy of The Immigrant Museum)

Town halls are prime examples of the care that was put into the design of public institutions during 'the glorious three decades' between 1945 and 1975. Designed by Arne Jacobsen with the landscape architect Eigil Kiær in 1954-56, Rødovre Town Hall is a gem of democratic welfare state architecture – a real 'people's palace'. Jacobsen also designed Aarhus Town Hall and Søllerød Town Hall. (Per Munkgård Thorsen/KADK DOCS)

Voldparken School designed by Kay Fisker in the neighbourhood Voldparken (1951-57) located close to Tingbjerg. (Kjeld de Fine Licht/KADK DOCS)

The high-rises of Milestedet in Rødovre and Brøndby municipalities, designed by various architects in 1956-1958, have contributed to making Vestegnen near Copenhagen famous for its landscape of towering concrete blocks. Here, one of the buildings by Svenn Eske Kristensen. (Tobias Faber/KADK DOCS)

A product of a collaboration between the famous landscape architect C. Th. Sørensen and Rødovre Municipality's city architect, Børge T. Lorentzen, the open-air bath Vestbadet is located in a green area between the high-rise housing estates of Milestedet and Nygårdsparken. Inaugurated in 1958, it is an example of the recreational and sports facilities constituting part of the dream scenario of the good life in the welfare city with its focus on the health and well-being of citizens enjoying their increased leisure time – not least the children. (C. Th. Sørensen/KADK DOCS)

It is fascinating to read the architect Steen Eiler Rasmussen's thoughts on the planning of Tingbjerg, a New Town built from scratch in the north-western part of Copenhagen. Under the banner of 'the human society', he describes the coming community in all its aspects, planned meticulously to satisfy the needs of a variety of new pioneer residents: the infants, the small children, the teenagers, the adults (working men and housewives) and the elderly. Many things went quite differently than planned and the residents later included migrants and refugees arriving from the late 1960s and onwards. Despite its beautiful brick architecture and organic landscape spaces, Tingbjerg is currently undergoing a major transformation dictated by the 'parallel society package'. Interventions such as densification with new housing typologies and the implementation of different kinds of ownerships are employed in an attempt to change the demographics of the area. In this perspective, reading Steen Eiler Rasmussen's thoughts on the future demography and everyday life of the New Town as formulated in 1963 provides a thought-provoking juxtaposition.

> 'In the Anglo-Saxon countries it has been considered as an ideal to have the city divided into so-called neighbourhoods. The neighbourhood-idea is a reaction against the 19th century's monstrous desert-like residential areas of identical streets and identical houses; the sad areas where the individual dwelling is merely a number amongst thousands of others, and where you would think that the residents must struggle to feel any affiliation with the area.
>
> It is desired to have the indistinct mass of houses splintered into smaller units, which should all be organized individually as a complete small town, a society apart. In particular, it is desired to avoid the large indistinct mass of people that all belong to the same social sphere. It is claimed that this will offer fundamentally different opportunities for the individual person when he interacts daily with people that have different jobs and viewpoints than himself. It would be useful if the intellectual worker could learn from the manual worker, rather than living segregated from one another.
>
> (...)
>
> Reality will probably turn out somewhat different from what the idealists have imagined. Experience shows that even if people from different population groups and different working areas live door by door, they do not interact much. Yet, it is important to avoid too

much uniformity. If a settlement or a part of a settlement becomes a sort of a ghetto for one particular and less regarded social group, it can exert considerable damage to the residents, not least the children (...) For the sake of the children and the youth coming of age one should therefore strive to create a district with a diversely composed population where, to the extent possible, all the different social layers of the city are represented, also different professions and different age groups.'

(Steen Eiler Rasmussen, 'Menneskesamfundet Tingbjerg', 1963 (*Arkitekten* 7, 2019, pp. 41-45)

ABOUT CHRISTIANIA

Rather surprisingly, the New Town planner and socially committed architect Steen Eiler Rasmussen, who planned Tingbjerg as an ideal city from tabula rasa, later became a defender of the then five-year old freetown of Christiania in a small book written in 1976. The abandoned military base in the middle of Copenhagen that was squatted by so-called 'slum stormers' in 1971, was quite a mind-blowing experience for Eiler Rasmussen. He admired how people managed to organize their own urban society from the bottom up without a master plan – a great contrast to the totally planned Tingbjerg, which developed into a much more rigid planning scheme than he had intended.

'It had been my dream that people would move to Tingbjerg from cramped conditions in the city to find larger spaces and grander freedom. And now I saw a warped picture of the plan: people placed in institutions according to time tables, where they could be controlled from cradle to grave (...) From Tingbjerg in one end of Copenhagen, where everything is quite heartlessly regulated and normalized and forced into the correct forms, one can get on bus number 8 and drive to the other end of Copenhagen, to Christiania, where everything is free, too free many believe.'

(Steen Eiler Rasmussen, *Omkring Christiania*, 1976, Copenhagen: Gyldendals Tranebøger, pp. 34-35)

Tingbjerg in the 1960s, photographed by the landscape architect C. Th. Sørensen, with whom Steen Eiler Rasmussen designed the New Town. (C. Th Sørensen/KADK DOCS)

Although Steen Eiler Rasmussen was operating on a vast scale when designing a completely New Town, he nevertheless carefully designed for different kinds of residents. This is apparent from the charming sketches accompanying his reflections on the coming community. (Steen Eiler Rasmussen, *Menneskesamfundet Tingbjerg*. Copenhagen: Steen Eiler Rasmussen's Office, 1963)

Penetrating the fence, squatters performatively declared the creation of the Freetown Christiania on 26 September 1971, before taking control of the abandoned military barracks on Christianshavn in the heart of Copenhagen. With a motley blend of reused old structures, new off-grid housing, undomesticated urban nature and self-sustained infrastructure and institutions, the flower children created their own alternative society. The success and future of the city-within-the-city is subject to debate. Over the years, Christiania has had its challenges, including drug-related crime, politicians wanting to kick the Christianites out, planners wanting to control construction on the ramparts, and, as in many other enclaves, aging is a factor. Nevertheless, it has survived against all odds for almost 50 years, its urban utopia offering inspiration for new initiatives and new ways of living and building in the otherwise carefully regulated city of Copenhagen. (Vilhelm Wohlert/KADK DOCS)

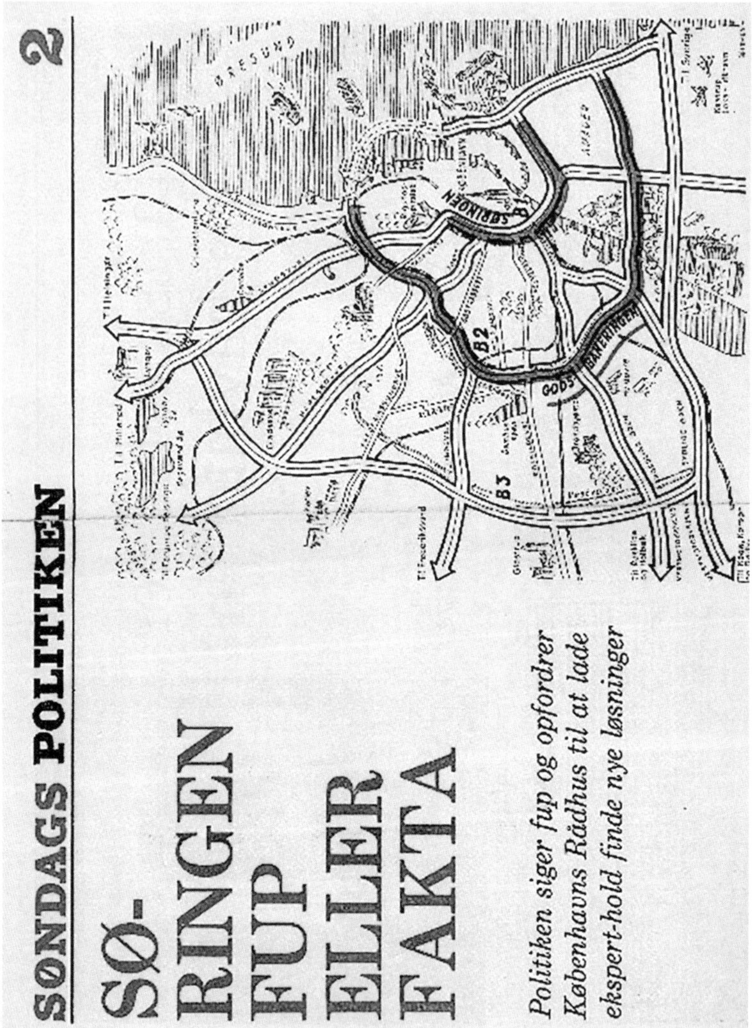

SØNDAGS **POLITIKEN** 2

SØ-RINGEN FUP ELLER FAKTA

Politiken siger fup og opfordrer Københavns Rådhus til at lade ekspert-hold finde nye løsninger

Front page of the Danish national newspaper Politiken, referenced from http://danishdesignreview.com/townscape/2017/9/5/sringen-a-motorway-along-the-lakes

One of the great unrealized modernist – and perhaps overly rational – visions for the city of Copenhagen was Søringen, or the Søgade project, a highway that would cut across the Lakes in the city centre. The project was first introduced in 1958 but met with opposition and was finally shelved in 1973 after protests from residents concerned about the effects it would have on their local environment.

> 'By the early 50s, the first drafts appeared for a motorway along Copenhagen's Lake Ring (Søring), a ring road connecting the main approaches in order to feed traffic from Greater Copenhagen into the inner city. The proposals met with some resistance, which was primarily motivated by urban aesthetics. The proposed, relatively sharp reduction of the lake area would reduce the significance of the Lakes, both architecturally and in their use. Among other considerations, it was feared that the residents inside the Søring would be cut off from accessing the Lakes. Later, the criticism against the proposal was reinforced based on a more technical city planning assessment. Why bring so much traffic into the inner city so that it was necessary to direct it via a ring road in order to avoid choking the city centre? At one point, the motorway along the Lakes had assumed such dimensions with enormous exit ramps that the large American motorway constructions were brought into mind.'

('Søgadeprojektet i ny udformning', *Arkitekten* 24, 1967)

PLANNING 100 YEARS AHEAD

Constantinos A. Doxiadis was a Greek urban planner who planned far more New Towns than his much more famous colleague Le Corbusier. With offices in 40 countries, he designed master plans in cities all over the world, including Islamabad, Sadr City in Baghdad, Detroit, Thema in Ghana etc. During a time of social engineering and 'planning fever', Doxiadis made his own 'science' of human settlements called 'Ekistics'. After a visit to Copenhagen in 1961, he was asked by the Danish journal *Arkitekten* to do a planning sketch for Greater Copenhagen. He presented (no less than) a 100-year plan, extending on the Finger Plan and suggesting that the centre of the ever expanding city of Copenhagen should be moved to Ringsted. This proposition was discussed and written extensively about in the national and local newspapers. In the heyday of top-down planning, it was allowed to think 100 years ahead, and the architect was given great authority and ability to predict future challenges and developments.

'The fact that I speak of the need to plan a hundred years ahead does not mean that we should build for a need we will have in 100 years. We will simply be prepared for the needs, and as the planning process progresses we will always have time to adjust our construction plans if they seem unrealistic in 10, 20, 30 or 40 years. What will happen to our plans when that time comes? (...) These are general observations that I have based on special studies in which I presume a growth of 12-30 billion, and where I very often speak of a median of 24 billion inhabitants on Earth in the last part of the next century. Even if we presume such a colossal population growth, Copenhagen will probably only have 5-5.5 million inhabitants.

(...)

It is quite likely that the old centre will preserve many of the functions that are of relevance to the immediate surroundings, to the city's administration and the tourists that will be more eager to visit the old areas of Copenhagen than the new – at least until we learn to build new cities that are just as beautiful and humane as the old. However, I cannot imagine that new shopping centres, supermarkets and so forth will be built in the old centre.

(...)

On the contrary, we must realize the necessity of creating entirely new centres to liberate our current big city centres from the pressure so that they can survive to the benefit of their inhabitants and to the benefit of the entire area.

WE MUST BECOME CITY BUILDERS RATHER THAN CITY SURGEONS.

One day mankind must learn that it cannot continuously build on the cities that have been handed over for generations, it must learn to build cities on the basis of experiences from the past. Let us exercize the courage to create for the future and not merely fight to change and remould the creations of the past. Why don't we dare to be forefathers to those who are to come – why are we merely satisfied with being the descendants of those who are gone?'

(C.A. Dioxiadis, 'Ja, en 100 års plan', *Arkitekten* 8, 1964, pp. 171-174)

Designed by Fællestegnestuen, Albertslund Syd constitutes an iconic masterplan. The low-dense environment, built between 1963-1968, mixes courtyard houses, terraced houses and low apartment blocks, a range of green spaces, separation between 'hard' and 'soft' road users and the 'spine' of a canal, adding local identity. Locating a shopping and community centre with welfare institutions close to the local S-train station, it is a clear example of a Finger Plan New Town experimenting with prefabricated building elements and facilitating new lifestyles in the welfare society on the rise. (Mogens Breyen /KADK Docs

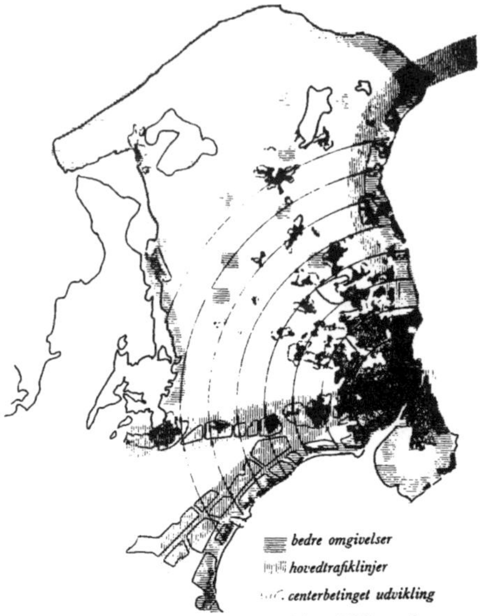

27. København år 2060. Nye bydannelser påvirker udviklingstendensen. Udviklingen mod bedre omgivelser. Udviklingen langs hovedårer. Udvikling mod en central lokalisering.

28. København år 2060. Større områder er nødvendige for at modtage den naturlige udvikling. Vandret skravering er udviklingsområder med smukke omgivelser. Lodret skravering er trafikalt betingede udviklingsområder.

In these maps Doxiadis sketches Copenhagen's possible urban growth by the year 2060 where large areas are necessary to encompass what he, according to the period's logic of eternal growth, calls 'natural evolution'. Thus, he incarnated the post-war architect/planner as a figure of engineer, doctor or prophet.

'First think, then act' was the headline of a discussion article by the architect and architectural critic Poul Erik Skriver, who was editor-in-chief of the Danish architectural journal *Arkitekten* for many years. Here, he reflects on Copenhagen's Lord Mayor Urban Hansen's plan for Vestamager that would continue all the way out to the suburbs. In line with the rationality of large-scale master plans and the so-called Prefab Circular, introduced by the Ministry of Housing in 1960, that increased the pace of residential construction significantly by making industrialized building methods mandatory, Hansen imagined a final plan that would eliminate housing shortage for good with 20,000 dwellings. Urbanplanen was indeed realized 1965-71, albeit on a much smaller scale than Hansen originally intended, providing housing for approximately 6,000 residents in 3,000 dwellings. Here, Skriver warns against the danger of too much rationality resulting in mindless repetitions of the same dwelling types dictated by technology and a one-size-fits-all logic. This debate is somewhat recognizable in the new urban neighbourhoods of today, where standard-size flats are repeated endlessly, and there is again a failure of adapting to different incomes and needs.

'No one knows better than the architect how painful it is to wait for years for the realization of a good idea. Urban Hansen has come up with the excellent idea to systematize the coming ten years of housing construction in Copenhagen and the city's plots in the surrounding municipalities. Overall, this simple idea has been well received and the Lord Mayor is eager to get started. A little too eager, perhaps. The project is considerably more complicated than the Lord Mayor grasped when he presented the idea. The foundation for such a large-scale activity must be well laid. The bigger the house, the more solid the foundation. The Urbanplan is not yet programmed. Regardless, the project is approached as if it were something that can be fixed along the way. It cannot. (...) Already by now, there are of course people working on the houses of the Urbanplan. The main idea of the Lord Mayor is the production plan, the dream of creating an assembly line production of dwellings. It is the industrialized element production and highly rationalized construction plans that are the goal. Increased productivity, greater output at the same cost, more and cheaper flats are the precise aim of the Lord Mayor. (...) If the houses that are to fill the construction plan prove to be soulless industrial products, the public will react strongly.'

(...)

'Danish housing construction has completely stagnated. The causes are easily identified. A stubborn maintenance of maximum sizes and maximum prices has inhibited any possibility for experimentation. The layouts used for prefabricated construction are not derived from industrialization. They are old floor plans that have been adapted to the new production methods. It is the heavy responsibility of politicians that Danish housing standards have lagged behind compared to developments in our neighbouring countries."

(Poul Erik Skriver, 'Først tænke – så handle', *Arkitekten* 3, 1964, pp. 169-170)

EVERYDAY LIFE IN THE MASTER PLAN

In the wake of the Danish government's current plans to transform social housing estates, the young author Morten Pape stimulated debate with his debut novel *The Plan* (*Planen*, 2015). In the novel, Pape describes his childhood and youth of the 1990s and 2000s in Urbanplanen and portrays the bittersweet everyday life in the multicultural Copenhagen enclave.

'The lady lived in the concrete social housing development Urbanplanen, the Urban Plan, that was named after then mayor Urban Hansen, who had conceived a grandiose plan about the future welfare architecture for ordinary Danish workers... Apart from the woodchip wallpaper walls of the terraced house, Urbanplanen had everything one could desire in a hopeful existence, and one never had to go far to find the most necessary. There were several washing facilities in the different areas named after old crafts such as basketmakers, chair makers, and hatters. There were nurseries and kindergartens as integrated parts of Urbanplanens socio-complete landscape package. A youth club was under construction on the other side of the large parking lot, and there was also a junk playground across from the little farm with goats, horses, a couple of hens and a single cow. There was a hill for sledding and ball courts, green areas and playgrounds in between the heavy housing blocks, on the central square across from the church and the school one could grocery shop, go to the pharmacy, take care of business in the Amager bank, send letters and packages at the post office, have a beer at the pub or ask for money for another round at the social security office.'

(Morten Pape, *Planen*. Copenhagen: Politikens Forlag, 2015, pp. 20-21)

A view of parts of Urbanplanen taken in 1970 from the newly constructed activity centre for senior residents, Peder Lykke Centeret, which at its opening was described as 'Northern Europe's most advanced care centre'. The centre intended to support an active and joyful old age that would keep Urbanplanen's senior residents involved in their community while also assisting them in everyday life so that they could stay in their own homes for as long as possible. (Kurt Andersen/VISDA)

POTEMKIN VILLAGES

The well-known Danish author Klaus Rifbjerg was a prophet of modernity and progress in his poetry and prose from the 1950s-1960s. Yet, in this interview he expresses his dislike of the modernist high-rises of Urbanplanen on Amager, where he lived as a child.

> 'Let me put it like this: Nostalgia isn't what it used to be. But of course, I can have a longing. On the other hand, it really isn't all modernity that is equally attractive. Urbanplanen isn't exactly something that one dreams about. We are living under the laws of change, but I am finding it difficult to accept when progress leads to something ugly. Ugly architecture, for instance. Those Potemkin villages that the harbour front has been boarded up with have emptied the area. Previously, it was alive with cranes and ships.'

(Klaus Rifbjerg quoted in Thomas Ambrosius, 'Over Rifbjergs broer', in *Jyllands-Posten*, 4 March 2006).

OUR FATHERS UP ABOVE!

In 1967, the young architect Jan Gehl wrote a polemical and critical article in the landscape architectural journal *Havekunst* on the new high-rises in Høje Gladsaxe – five enormous monoliths towering above the welfare city landscape. Gehl considered the everyday perspectives of different residents, and the text exemplifies how the feminist critique of the provider/housewife dichotomy of the normative gender balance is gradually kicking in. There is no doubt that the principles of the Prefab Circular, imposing prefab construction and the linearity of crane tracks, quantitatively improved the housing stock during a period in need of well-functioning and affordable housing. Nevertheless, these housing tactics created living environments that became increasingly criticized for being alienating 'concrete deserts' lacking in human scale.

> 'One can find Høje Gladsaxe, and one can find his/her way around Høje Gladsaxe. What remains is the question as to whether one can also live there. Not a word about flats, kitchen-dining-front rooms and problems of high-rise housing here, only an assessment of the living conditions in the significant part of the home, that which is outside the lift door, the place where "one" can move and exist when "one" doesn't want to be inside and can't leave the area because the cars have left and the bus connections are bad.

(...)

THE MOTHERS

The entire morning the flow leads away from Høje Gladsaxe. The cars take off as a flock of starlings from the parking lots and soon only the permanent stock is left, the approximately 2,000 mothers enslaved to the area by children and bad bus connections.

They are better off than suburban mothers in general. They have a centre. A shopping area with great activity, many good shops, a pastry shop followed by a string of service functions, conference rooms, cafeterias, etc.

(...)

The influx to the centre is vast. They all visit on a daily basis, not because the shopping can't be rationalized, but because one needs to do something. One makes a trip of it. 12 minutes each way for the fastest, 25 minutes each way if one brings the little ones along, and so one does.

The row of high-rises forms a spine in the consistently implemented pedestrian system, and on the way, whether it is short or long, one has as many as three routes to choose from.
Route A, 650 meters of straight asphalt to the north of the high-rises with parking – garages – parking – garages – parking etc. on one side, and to the other high-rise – washing facility – high-rise – washing facility – high-rise etc.

(...)

THE FATHERS

Imagine being able to start the day by watching the sun rise above the capital, being able to go to work in the inner city, in Roskilde or in Malmö and still be able to see all the way home to the omnipresent row of shining white houses where mommy dearest and the children are having a cosy time. To come home and be surrounded by happy, playing children already in the parking lot and then rise up above to peace, calm, dinner and the sunset over Storebælt. Høje Gladsaxe must be a wonderful place to live, a great, great sleeping city for that quarter of residents that only need to sleep in the area.

Naturally, weekends and holidays pose problems but collective car washing in the garage yards combined with excursions, visits and holiday houses solves many of these problems. Probably, the leisurely landscape in Høje Gladsaxe puts strain on the country roads, but on a daily basis Høje Gladsaxe must be something close to the ideal place to live – for fathers.

The sensation intensifies as one gets to know the settlement. This area is built and designed as a supplement to an otherwise eventful and active daily life. It is built by fathers – for fathers.

(...)

It is the less privileged – the homeworkers, the old and the small ones that see their opportunities reduced. They pay the price for Høje Gladsaxe not having become a living city in a beautiful landscape but rather having become – well – a monument for the patriarchal society.'

(Jan Gehl, 'Vore fædre i det høje', Havekunst 7 1967: Nordisk tidsskrift for planlægning af have og landskab (special issue on Høje Gladsaxe), The Danish Architectural Press)

Situated close to the beautiful nature reserve of Utterslev Mose, Høje Gladsaxe's skyline of five 16-storey monoliths, brutalistically arranged on a straight row, is truly iconic. At the time, this industrialized prefab development, erected 1963-66 and designed by architects Jørgen Juul Møller, Kai Agertoft, Alex Poulsen and Hoff & Windinge with the landscape architects Sven Hansen, Mogens Klint and Andreas Bruun, was cutting edge. The housing complex also comprises two 9-storey blocks and some lower housing. In addition, there are a school, three daycare centres, a community centre, two youth clubs, a senior centre, a church, a library and a shopping centre. The Gladsaxe Plan was the brainchild of Gladsaxe's passionate Social Democratic mayor Erhard Jakobsen, who joined the Danish parliament in 1973 with his new party, the Centrum-Democraterne, fuelled by a new social awareness after the stagnation of the economic welfare boom.(C. Th. Sørensen, Hoff & Windinge, Tobias Faber, Andreas Trier Mørch/ KADK DOCS)

The welfare city also fostered new consumer patterns in a Keynesian economy where socialism and capitalism shook hands. This new consumer lifestyle as an integrated part of the everyday suburban life is visible in Rødovre Centrum, Denmark's first covered mall, which opened in 1966. While many other suburban open air shopping cum community centres are today slowly suffocating, following the success of new hypermarkets within driving distance, Rødovre Centrum is still quite popular and has been renovated and expanded several times. (C. Th. Sørensen/KADK DOCS)

Aerial photograph of Taastrupgaard – one of the largest social housing estates in Denmark, realized in 1972. The area is currently undergoing a major transformation with demolitions and the addition of new housing structures according to the principles of the so-called Ghetto Plan that aims to balance the social mix of the neighbourhood as well as the wider Høje Taastrup Municipality. (Aerial photo by unknown photographer/KADK DOCS)

One of the cornerstones of the welfare city is of course the architecture of welfare institutions, which take care of the citizens' health and well-being from cradle to grave. Kindergartens, libraries, schools, hospitals, nursing homes, universities, job centres etc.

Designed by architects Gehrdt Bornebusch, Max Brüel and Jørgen Selchau with the landscape architect Sven Hansen, the 26-storey high-rise Herlev Hospital, inaugurated in 1976, is one of the monuments of Brutalism in a Danish context. (Kjeld de Fine Licht/KADK DOCS)

Art played a major role in the welfare state. Democratization of and access to artworks of high quality were part of the dream of the good and fulfilling life in the post-class society. As such, art was part of the plan to educate and socially elevate ordinary people – not least members of the working class. Moreover, it was integrated in the design of public spaces and welfare institutions. A prime examples is Poul Gernes' work at Herlev Hospital – a colourful explosion inside an otherwise brutalist monolith in greyish concrete. For decades, it has been debated whether to keep the site-specific artwork and whether it actually benefits the well-being of the patients. (Camilla Hedegaard Møller)

With its strictly geometrical lines, rough concrete and sheer volume the Panum Institute (built 1970–86), accommodating the medical faculty of the University of Copenhagen, is a brutalist landmark in Copenhagen. The loved and hated building was designed by the architect couple Nils and Eva Koppel, who worked for Alvar Aalto and also designed the university institutions of DTU (Technical University of Denmark) and KUA, the now demolished humanities branch of the University of Copenhagen. (Sandra Gonon/KADK DOCS)

Back in 1971, architect Jan Gehl wrote the modern classic *Life Between Buildings,* advocating for the human scale and the social aspects of architecture and urbanism, while urging fellow professionals to consider the importance of creating good conditions for the life that unfolds between buildings. From being part of a minor grassroots practice, inspired by urban activists like Jane Jacobs and Kevin Lynch, protesting against regeneration of existing neighbourhoods, demolitions and the modernists' large-scale master plans, Jan Gehl's theories have become almost common sense in the planning profession. Today, cities all over the globe are consulting the still active architect for advice on how to improve local urban environments. Moreover, Gehl has coined the hyped urban concept of liveability.

ACTIVE PARTICIPATION OR PASSIVE CONSUMPTION

'It is hardly a coincidence that criticism of functionalism, of the new urban areas, and of the sprawling suburbs primarily has been directed specifically toward the neglected, the destroyed, and the missing public spaces (...) The automobile has made it possible to replace active participation in spontaneous local social activities with a drive to see selected friends and attractions. Abundant possibilities do exist for compensating for what has been lost. Precisely for this reason, the fact that there is still widespread criticism of the neglected public spaces is indeed thought provoking. Something is missing. That something is missing is illustrated emphatically by widespread popular protests against physical planning as it is practiced, evidenced in debates on city and residential environments and the organization of residents around demands for improvement of the physical environment. Typical demands include better conditions for pedestrian and bicycle traffic, better conditions for children and the elderly and a better framework in general for recreational and social community function.'

(Jan Gehl, *Life Between Buildings: Using Public Space*, 1971 (2011), London: Island Press)

The architects of the architectural office Vandkunsten were pioneers in housing design with their concept of 'dense-low', two-storey row houses with gardens as an alternative to – or combination of – the high-rise and the single family house. It was a 2.0 version of the post-1968 welfare city, where the users became involved in the building process. Local democracy and community were key. Below is an excerpt of Vandkunsten's almost manifesto-like and Marxism-inspired project from 1972 that won the low-dense competition held by the Danish Building Research Institute in 1971.

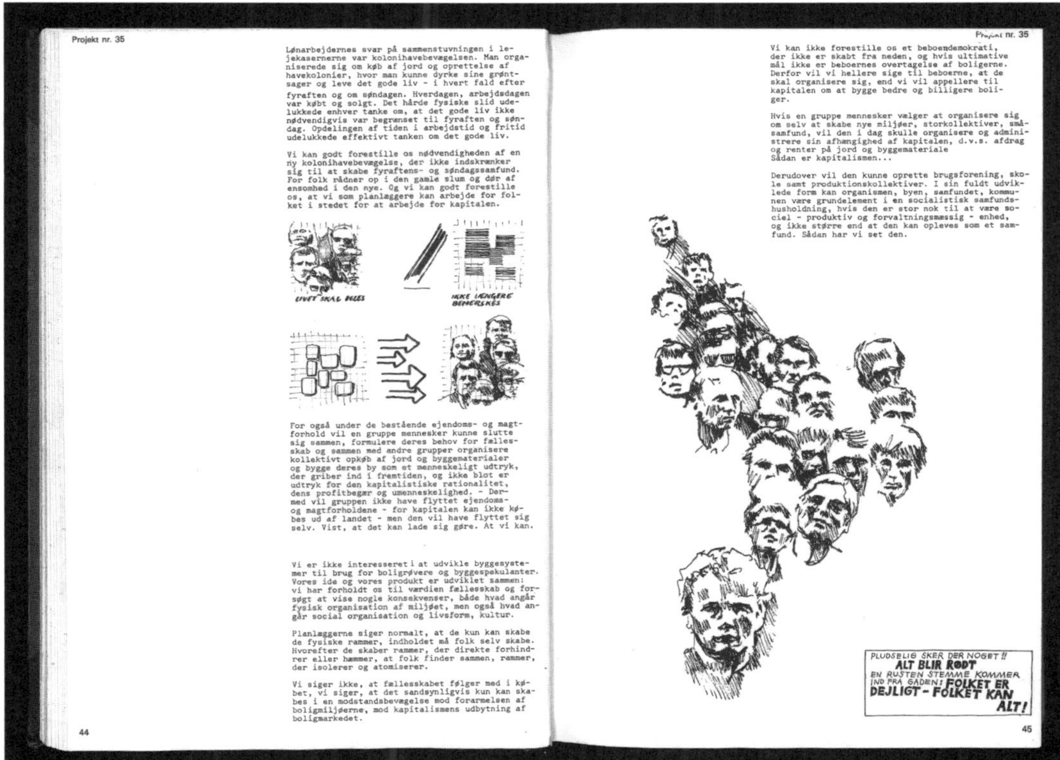
Projekt nr. 35

Lønarbejdernes svar på sammenstuvningen i lejekasernerne var kolonihavebevægelsen. Man organiserede sig om køb af jord og oprettelse af havekolonier, hvor man kunne dyrke sine grøntsager og leve det gode liv - i hvert fald efter fyraften og om søndagen. Hverdagen, arbejdsdagen var købt og solgt. Det hårde fysiske slid udelukkede enhver tanke om, at det gode liv ikke nødvendigvis var begrænset til fyraften og søndag. Opdelingen af tiden i arbejdstid og fritid udelukkede effektivt tanken om det gode liv.

Vi kan godt forestille os nødvendigheden af en ny kolonihavebevægelse, der ikke indskrænker sig til at skabe fyraftens- og søndagssamfund. For folk rådner op i den gamle slum og dør af ensomhed i den nye. Og vi kan godt forestille os, at vi som planlæggere kan arbejde for folket i stedet for at arbejde for kapitalen.

For også under de bestående ejendoms- og magtforhold vil en gruppe mennesker kunne slutte sig sammen, formulere deres behov for fællesskab og sammen med andre grupper organisere kollektivt opkøb af jord og byggematerialer og bygge deres by som et menneskeligt udtryk, der griber ind i fremtiden, og ikke blot er udtryk for den kapitalistiske rationalitet, dens profitbegær og umenneskelighed. - Dermed vil gruppen ikke have flyttet ejendoms- og magtforholdene - for kapitalen kan ikke købes ud af landet - men den vil have flyttet sig selv. Vist, at det kan lade sig gøre. At vi kan.

Vi er ikke interesseret i at udvikle byggesystemer til brug for boligrøvere og byggespekulanter. Vores ide og vores produkt er udviklet sammen: vi har forholdt os til værdien fællesskab og forsøgt at vise nogle konsekvenser, både hvad angår fysisk organisation af miljøet, men også hvad angår social organisation og livsform, kultur.

Planlæggerne siger normalt, at de kun kan skabe de fysiske rammer, indholdet må folk selv skabe. Hvorefter de skaber rammer, der direkte forhindrer eller hæmmer, at folk finder sammen, rammer, der isolerer og atomiserer.

Vi siger ikke, at fællesskabet følger med i købet, vi siger, at det sandsynligvis kun kan skabes i en modstandsbevægelse mod forarmelsen af boligmiljøerne, mod kapitalismens udbytning af boligmarkedet.

44

Projekt nr. 35

Vi kan ikke forestille os et beboerdemokrati, der ikke er skabt fra neden, og hvis ultimative mål ikke er beboernes overtagelse af boligerne. Derfor vil vi hellere sige til beboerne, at de skal organisere sig, end vi vil appellere til kapitalen om at bygge bedre og billigere boliger.

Hvis en gruppe mennesker vælger at organisere sig om selv at skabe nye miljøer, storkollektiver, småsamfund, vil den i dag skulle organisere og administrere sin afhængighed af kapitalen, d.v.s. afdrag og renter på jord og byggemateriale
Sådan er kapitalismen...

Derudover vil den kunne oprette brugsforening, skole samt produktionskollektiver. I sin fuldt udviklede form kan organismen, byen, samfundet, kommunen være grundelement i en socialistisk samfundshusholdning, hvis den er stor nok til at være social - produktiv og forvaltningsmæssig - enhed, og ikke større end at den kan opleves som et samfund. Sådan har vi set den.

45

(Courtesy of Vandkunsten)

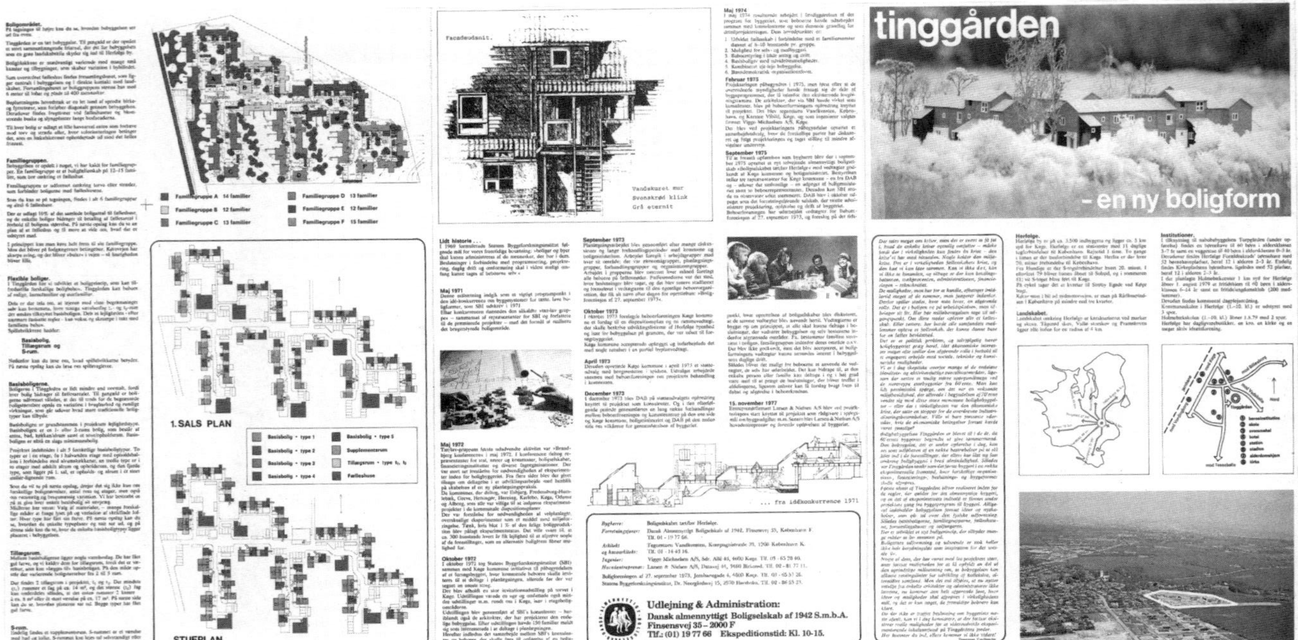

As a second generation welfare city, Tinggården was planned in the wake of 1968 where local community and human scale were key. Novelties included the possibility of citizen participation in the design process, decentralized resident democracy and expression of individuality through a more self-grown and informal add-on architecture and a variety of building materials. Emerging out of the aforementioned low-dense competition in 1971, Tinggården was built in two phases – Tinggården I was completed in 1978 and Tinggården II in 1982. The area is divided into family groups of 12-18 flats in houses organized around a central square or alley. Each group has a communal house for communal dinner and other activities. Today, Tinggården has become a leading international example of a successful housing complex with an element of community and local democracy. This flyer presents the new housing community and social lifestyle, 'recruiting' pioneers to get involved in the design process and local democracy of the future Tinggården. (Courtesy of Vandkunsten)

The neighbourhood Galgebakken in Albertslund (1972-74) constitutes a rethinking of the single-family house (parcelhuset), which became popular towards the end of the 1960s and the beginning of the 1970s, as well as a reconceptualization of social housing. With its fluid boundaries between public and private space and its emphasis on shared social environments, it attracted many young progressive families who, amongst other initiatives, organized a local cooperative society with a small grocery store. A small city within the town of Albertslund, the development features a combination of communal areas, flexible path systems and small housing communities organized along narrow lanes of about ten houses each. The houses have private back gardens and open front gardens with wide glass doors facing the neighbours but neither gates nor fences. (J. P. Storgård, Jørn Ørum Nielsen, Hanne Marcussen, Anne Ørum Nielsen's office/KADK DOCS)

Farum Midtpunkt was designed as an experimental prefab system by Jørn Ole Sørensen, Viggo Møller-Jensen and Tyge Arnfred, and built between 1972 and 1975. The terraced housing development is famous for combining the flat and the row house. In line with the Zeitgeist, community was a core value. You could enjoy the privacy of the single-family house while interacting with other residents in the indoor walkways that also connected various communal spaces. Some flats are designed particularly as family dwellings and spread over two floors. All units have access to a private terrace. (Tobias Faber/KADK DOCS)

In addition to Jorn and the Situationists, there are many examples of counter culture and grassroots initiatives that rethought architecture and urbanism in an activist way according to post-1968 and punk-squatter bottom-up ideals of free expression and DIY.

1970 was the summer of love in North Jutland. Inspired by Woodstock and other hippie initiatives, the association of the New Society (Det Nye Samfund), founded in 1968 in Copenhagen, bought 47 acres of land in Han Herred near Frøstrup and realized their utopian dreams during a 73-day summer camp. Among the rather romantic crowd were the young architects Carsten Hoff and Susanne Ussing, who built experimental structures for emancipated co-living in the new society with its redefinitions of norms and lifestyles. Along with other countermoves against the (over)planned and rather conformist modernist housing estates, such initiatives challenged the one-size-fits-all logic of top-down planning. Part of the experimental community still prevails today with around 70 permanent residents and a host of hangers-on. (Andreas Trier Mørch/KADK DOCS)

Poster from the fight against the demolition of the adventure playground ‘Byggeren’ (the Builder) from 1972–80 in the blue-collar neighbourhood of Nørrebro. ‘Byggeren’ was established by local residents on a gigantic empty plot which emerged during the big redevelopments in the late 1960s and early 1970s. While municipal construction plans were put on hold, the residents took action, and in 1974 they persuaded the municipality to recognize ‘Byggeren’ as a municipal institution and save it from future redevelopment. Yet in 1978, the new Lord Mayor Egon Weidekamp and KBI (Cooperative Building Industry) launched a new plan for a dense new housing project, nicknamed ‘Egon’s Plan’. After many confrontations between the locals and the municipality, the police moved in, and in March 1980 bulldozers finally demolished and vacated the playground. As a result, the squatter movement BZ-bevægelsen that grew out of the 1960s’ and 70s’ slum stormers, stepped up its actions. Throughout the 1980s, BZ-bevægelsen squatted several buildings in the districts of Nørrebro and Vesterbro, leading to numerous intense confrontations with the police. (Public domain via wiki)

Unlike Copenhagen's current prosperity and success in the interurban competition with 10,000 incomers per year, the Danish capital was on the verge of bankruptcy around 1990. The migration pattern and demography was very different back then, as those who could afford it typically moved out of the socio-economically challenged and deindustrializing capital to single-family houses in the suburbs. As a response, the municipality mobilized a number of strategies, aiming to halt this exodus of the middle class while attracting investors, tourists and more resourceful tax-payers to Copenhagen. One strategy to upgrade the capital was to regenerate historical districts such as the working class neighbourhoods of Nørrebro and Vesterbro, making it more attractive for middle-class families to reside in Copenhagen. Gradually, this boosted the real estate market and changed the demography. As Copenhagen became the European Capital of Culture in 1996, new venues like Vega opened, and public spaces like Skt. Hans Torv became popular places to enjoy an expensive coffee. The municipality also began branding Copenhagen as a 'liveable' and saleable city in order to attract the segment that the urbanist Richard Florida would later dub 'the creative class'. Yet another strategy to tackle the crises was the planning of the New Town Ørestad on Amager Fælled, a tabula rasa project strategically placed close to Copenhagen Airport and thus connected to an international network of cities on the rise in a global neoliberal economy. Ørestad was also fundamental to securing funding for the new metro, a financial strategy for infrastructural development that would come to dictate the development of the city in the following decades.

> 'Copenhagen has reached the agenda of the parliament. The stagnating metropolis must rebuild some of the force that it lost during the efforts to rectify the crooked Denmark. Words like dynamo, locomotive etc. express this dream of growth.
>
> (...)
>
> Copenhagen has been on a deroute. To that extent the national planning succeeded. The crooked Denmark has been rectified – yes, has healed to the detriment of Copenhagen. However, the problems of Copenhagen have clear international parallels. Large american cities such as New York, Chicago and others were on the brink of bankruptcy until the mid 80s from virtually the same reasons. The big city works like a magnet – also on the socially weak, and the increasing burdens result in higher tax burdens. The wealthy flee. The city degenerates, the best tax payers leave etc., etc. This vicious circle must be broken. However, it isn't just external plagues that make Copenhagen

struggle. The critics are to some extent right when they claim that the municipal administration of Copenhagen is sluggish ...'

(Kim Dirckinck-Holmfeld, 'København', *Arkitekten* 6, 1990, p. 181)

ECHOING MODERNISM

The winning team of the 1995 Ørestad competition was a group of Finnish architects: Hannu Tikka, Yrjö Rossi, Teemu Palo, Matti Kaijansinkko and Aaro Artto. Here, they explain the concept of the debated plan that due to its zoning and linearity was criticized by some for being a remnant of modernist principles. The new neighbourhood eventually ended up as a weak echo of modernist planning.

INTRODUCTION TO THE ARCHITECTURAL CONCEPT

'The starting point was a long piece of green paper crossed by a red line representing the coming metro. "Design a plan good enough to be the basis for a city. Then we will sell the property under the city and pay for the metro."

On a long narrow site we designed a proposal for a city as a large garden to which we added roads, canals and parks. Between the parks we retained areas of the existing natural landscape. In time, the city will fill out the site and there will be a dynamic tension between the park and city.

If the city does not grow, there will be a tension between the open areas and the parks. In this way the future city will be stamped as a negative feature in our garden.

We attempt to set as high an architectural standard as possible. Our design strategy is to find an archetype that not only refers to itself and its style but also is elevated above that which could be considered typical of the time – a form idiom that appeals to our collective or cultural consciousness.'

(Hannu Tikka, Yrjö Rossi, Teemu Palo, Matti Kaijansinkko and Aaro Artto, 'Ørestaden', *Arkitektur DK* 45, 1996, p. 315)

Ørestaden as presented by the Finnish office APRT in 1995. (APRT)

The 'new' New Town Ørestad. (Andreas Trier Mørch/KADK DOCS)

NOT A WORD ABOUT ØRESTAD

Arne Gaardmand, one of the grand old men in Danish urban planning, was not satisfied with Ørestad – neither with what it does to the landscape nor the entire planning process.

> 'The Ørestad project is a provoking exertion of power and growthlust. A real need for the neighbourhood has never been demonstrated. It crops one of the capital's most valuable green areas. The plan is created clandestinely and is sought completed with mafia-like methods (...) Yet the powerful women and men behind the Ørestad project continue as if everything was fine and the critics a bunch of derouted babblers. A state-run Ørestad company is established with affiliated staff and a council "that possesses expertise within culture and nature" (...) In particular, I found it hard when the vision of a Ørestad of 5 kilometers in length and 500 meters in width emerged during the reading. But that was probably an entirely mistaken conflation from my side.'
>
> (Arne Gaardmand, 'Ikke et ord om Ørestaden', *Arkitekten* 10, 1994 , pp. 340-341)

THE 1990S' RENEWAL OF COPENHAGEN

Urban renewal and renovation of the existing building stock were elements of the welfare city that took place in parallel to the construction of new neighbourhoods and modern dwellings. Part of Copenhagen's urban fabric in the inner city and 'bridge' districts consisted of tiny, slummy flats with no toilet or shower. Not least Social Democratic politicians with a blue-collar background who had themselves been raised under such conditions were eager advocates of the transformation of old tenements and construction of new and modern dwellings to improve the quality of life for ordinary people. But more than anything, this urban renewal was a strategy to attract affluent taxpayers to come settle in the then relatively poor municipality of Copenhagen.

> 'the majority of the politicians – spearheaded by the Social Democrats and for a while also the Communists – prefered the "consistent" over-all solutions, and the leading bureaucrats were often of the same opinion. But that was mainly due to politicians such as Urban Hansen, Egon Weidekamp, Helge Nielsen and Anker Jørgensen having grown up in the slum (or at least knowing it well), and that they

had mixed blood in their youth and promised one another that they would fight for a real renewal of these areas. We academics and newcomers shouldn't turn up and orate on the idyll and resource efficiency of the loo in the backyard. It just had to go – and the residents of the bridge districts should be granted part in the housing benefits of the welfare society.'

(Arne Gaardmand, *Byfornyelse, fra gadegennembrud til integreret byfornyelse*, 10th seminar, June 1995, Gammel Dok, Copenhagen. Dansk Byplanlaboratorium)

IN DEFENSE OF CRITICAL DIALOGUE

In a comment from 1997, Jan Christiansen, who later became the city architect of Copenhagen, challenges the consensus he believes surrounds a new law on urban regeneration. He demands more critical dialogue in line with the spirit of the 1970s and the recently groomed city of Barcelona, which he has just visited.

'(...) today it is just as thought-provoking to what poor extent societal issues generate contradictory discussions, and how much consensus actually occurs on a general level. (...) In spite of the consensus and support for the proposed new laws, a debate exists concerning urban renewal and architecture, a debate which in Copenhagen concerns delicate issues such the Royal Theatre, the City Hall Square, infill housing projects, the Architects' House (!), and across the nation equally relevant issues. Conversations and experiences from a recently held study trip to Barcelona reveal that precisely those interventions in the city, the squares, and the parks that we have admired over the past decade, have now become subjected to intense popular and political critique – yes, even from the architectural profession. (...) Such a debate on architecture and city planning is vital and must be sustained with both literary and built contributions. And it seems as if we will have an urban renewal law that will make it possible also for works of architecture to occupy their well-deserved place in the city as beautiful, communicative, contemporary as well as dangerous and inappropriate.'

(Jan Christiansen and Leif Leer Sørensen, 'Byfornyelse 1997', *Arkitekten* 10, 1997)

That these previous initiatives of transformation are affecting the transformation initiatives of the present, e.g. on Nørrebro, is not surprising. Here, Arne Gaardmand recalls the urban conflicts on Nørrebro that arose in the wake of the demolition of the popular adventure playground 'Byggeren' in 1980, providing space for the construction of new social housing. Gaardmand highlights the collective memories of the project's top-down planning initiative as important and relevant factors to consider in the mid-1990s' urban renewal of the same neighbourhood.

> 'Inner Nørrebro is on the one hand a wonderful place to live ... we have shops, pubs, restaurants, shared facilities and green areas on a scale and of a quality that no other of the older districts in Copenhagen can match. On the other hand, there are at times conflicts and unpleasant tensions – both amongst the residents and in our relation to the remaining parts of the capital. This isn't so much caused, as some people believe, by the semi-boring and repetitive newly built houses. Rather it is probably caused by a failed politics of relocation, housing and social issues. And also to a large extent the heritage of unpleasant memories that Nørrebro carries with it from when the neighbourhood's transformation and renewal was executed.
>
> It is still vividly recollected on Nørrebro (if not by other means, then at least mythologically) how the plans were forced through, what little influence the citizens had and the extent to which the politicians, public servants and "the system" as a whole manifested governmental overreach and "only we know" attitudes. In extreme and tragic form when Byggeren (ed. a junk playground) was eradicated around May 1, 1980 – from the assistance of 800 battle-clad police officers, a large number of builders and several bulldozers. (...) There is also a critique against the urban renewal's inability to find its place in the social changes, from which it is created and to a large extent influences. Is it fair, it is being asked, having a resource demanding intervention that leads to very expensive housing in areas with many young, single, unemployed and receivers of social benefits.'
>
> (Arne Gaardmand, *Byfornyelse, fra gadegennembrud til integreret byfornyelse*, 10th seminar, June 1995, Gammel Dok, Copenhagen, Dansk Byplanlaboratorium)

Tense days in 1980 with confrontations between local residents and users of the junk playground 'Byggeren' and the police forces that were deployed to ensure that demolition teams could enter and tear it down to prepare the plot for new housing construction. The users and residents defended and barricaded the playground for almost a month, thus preventing builders from accessing the site to commence the demolition. In response, the municipality asked for police forces to be deployed. There were battles in the Nørrebro neighbourhood between civilian defenders of the playground and the police for several weeks. On May 5th, an estimated 10,000-15,000 Copenhageners gathered in protest, marching to the City Hall to demand that the playground was saved; however, a few days later, while the Nørrebro neighbourhood was declared to be under a state of exception, the playground was irreversibly bulldozed. 'Byggeren' was established by local residents in 1973, but in 1979 a municipal master plan proposing demolition to make space for new social housing was adopted. Today, the area, known as Sorte Firkant, the Black Square, is struggling with a variety of social challenges. (Photos by Søren Dyck-Madsen)

On 1 March 2007, The Youth House ('Ungeren') was cleared of people during a spectacular police action with helicopters after long-time resistance and street fights between the young autonomous activists and the police. Once again, Nørrebro was on fire, and the local Copenhageners were caught in the middle. In 1982, the alternative and rather anarchist Youth House was established in the former Assembly Hall of the Workers on Jagtvej 69 on Nørrebro in Copenhagen, where Rosa Luxemburg once met fellow revolutionaries, and the International Women's Day was founded in 1910 during the Second International Socialist Women's Congress. In 1982, the house was given to BZ-bevægelsen by the Copenhagen Municipality as an attempt to ease the conflicts following the demolition of the playground 'Byggeren'. In 2000, the municipality sold the building to HUMAN A/S, owned by the Christian sect of the Father House. The youth using the house refused to leave and legal and street battles ensued until the eviction in 2007. After the eviction, the religious group demolished the house. The users of 'Ungeren' were given another house on Dorotheavej, and the empty plot on Jagtvej is now used for guerrilla gardening and experiments with housing for homeless. (Wikipedia, Public domain)

RITT'S AFFORDABLE HOUSING

When the high-profile Social Democrat Ritt Bjerregaard became Lord Mayor of Copenhagen in 2006 after a long career in the Danish Folketing and the European Parliament, it was with an election pledge of building 5,000 affordable dwellings in five years. Dwellings for ordinary citizens – the nurse, the policeman, the teacher etc. – for whom it was becoming increasingly difficult to find affordable housing in the Danish capital. In the end, only twelve affordable dwellings were built in Sydhavnen, proving how difficult social initiatives were to realize in a time of construction craze and rocketing real estate prices in the years prior to the financial crisis in 2008.

'"Since I announced my candidacy in the autumn, I have said that it's completely amiss there is no housing in Copenhagen that is affordable to ordinary people. I have now tried to solidify this into something concrete," says Ritt Bjerregaard "I have felt obliged to present something very concrete that can be executed within the timespan of a single election period."

Ritt Bjerregaard doesn't conceal that she doesn't think much of the very costly housing that has sprung up in recent years in several places in Copenhagen, for instance the area by Langelinie and in Frihavnen.

"They will become dead districts void of life. What is exciting about the city, is precisely the mix."'

(Ritt Bjerregaard interviewed by Kristian Klarskov, 'Ritt Bjerregaard vil bygge 5.000 billige boliger', *Politiken*, April 2005)

Central to Ritt Bjerregaard's ambition of building 5,000 new affordable dwelling units in Copenhagen was Bjarke Ingels' proposal for the Kløvermarken plot. The project proposed to encircle the vast green space with a winding 'Chinese wall' structure comprising 3,000 units, thereby preserving most of the existing sports fields within the centre of the structure. The proposal polarized Copenhageners with 49 percent in favour and 51 percent against, according to a newspaper survey. Bjarke Ingels himself initiated a petition in an attempt to build momentum for the project, but, after a period of heated public debate, it was scrapped in 2007 by the city council. (Reference of BIG's project from Berlingske 11 November 2005, https://www.berlingske.dk/samfund/hvad-nu-hvis-amager-fik-kinesisk-mur-af-boliger accessed 3 March 2020)

Bjarke Ingels' old office PLOT, with the fellow partner Julien de Smedt, designed the Harbour Bath that opened in 2003. It is located close to part of Copenhagen's old industrial harbour on Islands Brygge where, among others, the Soy-Bean Factory used to pollute Amager. Along with Noma and biking, the Harbour Bath has become instrumental to Copenhagen's brand of a liveable, generous and hedonistic city with surplus value and room for leisure along the post-industrial harbour front. In the post-Fordist age, the clean swimming water has become part of the narrative of the clean and groomed city that rose from poverty. It is free and accessible to all with a capacity of 600 bathers. The dream of the good life 2.0 come true at a point when the Richard Florida-inspired *The Creative City* was still in fashion, and before Instagram and the recession in 2008. (Rasmus Hjortshøj)

In 2011, the journalist Pernille Stensgaard wrote an article on the then much debated phenomenon of 'liveability nausea', an expression coined as a reaction against new urban parks like BIG's Superkilen and the kind of sports playgrounds that favour the fit and active (wo)men while leaving behind the 'lazy' and old who simply wanted a bench to sit on and something green to enjoy. The new conceptualizations of public parks represented a more individualistic way of designing public spaces than the open-ended and perhaps more inclusive public spaces of the post-war period. The new projects also became important elements in the branding narrative of Copenhagen, voted 'the most liveable city' by lifestyle magazines such as *Monocle.*

> 'Superkilen is at once overwhelmingly different and overwhelmingly a product of its time. So fierce, artificial and kitsch that one struggles to call it a park. Parks are carefully planned breathing spaces created for calm and peace, bird song, the tree, the flower and the smell of dirt. This one is "a project" which people have to fill with meaning themselves. One definitely must not think of the place as finished and organized although it seems extremely finished and organized. When Superkilen still feels familiar it is because it, aside from the multicultural, also aims directly for the body. Everyone does that. All over the country there are new installations and city districts driven by the same urge to activate people in game playing and sweating. Not a week passes without a press release of the type: "an area of 19,200 square metres in Fanø is now activated with urban and landscape elements for culture and sports."
>
> A small hesitation is beginning to form. One of the country's leading landscape architects and urban space figures, professo r Stig L. Andersson, is getting close to an urban life nausea and imagines a future with more stress relieving nature in the city, more quiet and a complete absence of events. Approximately the opposite of the current city-life bombardment. The ordinary city, the old people's city, the quiet nature lovers' city, or the happily lazy people's city isn't just around the corner either.'
>
> (Pernille Stensgaard, 'Midt i Storbylegestuen', *Weekendavisen*, 3 February 2012)

The intention of the park/urban square Superkilen was to make a new meeting place by reinventing the identity and stimulating interaction in the socially mixed and challenged neighbourhood of Outer Nørrebro, close to the ghetto-listed social housing estate Mjølnerparken. Opening in 2011, Superkilen by architects BIG and Topotek 1 has famously incorporated urban furniture from all over the world in order to enhance the multicultural nature of the local neighbourhood; a process involving the artist collective Superflex, who invited residents to choose their favourite objects, such as a Japanese play octopussy, Brazilian benches, a boxing ring from Thailand, earth from Palestine etc. In this sense, the urban park/square reflects the 2010s' ethos of co-creation and citizen participation, although it has been debated how inclusive and democratic the participation process really was. (Unknown photographer/KADK DOCS)

Originating from 1934 and spanning parts of both Copenhagen and Tårnby municipalities, the public beach Amager Strandpark is one of the biggest welfare city projects of public space in Copenhagen. Particularly after Hasløv & Kjærsgaard's upgrading in 2004–05 with a new 2-km artificial island with beaches, fairway and dunes, the urban beach, the 'rambla' and the parks 5-Øren and 10-Øren have become a popular hangout and meeting place for Copenhageners as well as tourists, spanning from Turkish families barbecuing, over skaters and joggers, to swimmers dipping in the sea. (Andreas Trier Mørch KADK DOCS)

2.

Status

The utopian visions of collective happiness from cradle to grave and good housing for everybody in modernist suburbs and social housing estates have developed quite differently than planned during the post-war period. Today, the effects and experiences found in the rubbles of modernist urban planning are a hot topic among urbanists all over the world. Increasingly, professionals have to deal with rethinking or transforming the existing structures and contexts of sites with an everyday life, narrative and culture rather than mainly planning new tabula rasas. Both in scale and scope, the architecture and urbanism after 1945 are very present as cultural heritage and legacy. The sheer number of additions to the built environment constructed between 1945 and 1975 by far exceeds all previous periods. Thus, the basic aspirations and the social commitment of the modernist era seem more relevant than ever: through rational principles of construction and the celebration of aesthetic ideals, it is probably possible to solve the mounting challenges of our era, as urbanization across the globe is increasing rapidly, while inequality is on the rise. Creating a planning framework and supplying housing and New Town planning for billions of people across the planet demands the kind of discipline capable of grasping the enormity of the challenge.

Yet, unlike in the early modern era, i.e. between 1920 and 1940, the market-driven city is prevailing today. Cities like Copenhagen and Aarhus are competing with other cities around the world to attract the 'right' kind of citizens, investments, companies and tourists. As the influence of the ideology of the welfare state is losing momentum, the market has taken its place as the main driver of urban development. As a result, real estate prices are skyrocketing, while locals and first-time buyers have a hard time finding a place to live in the city. In addition, this is visible in the paradigm shift from a welfare state planning, which is mainly guided by the state and the municipality, towards a more neoliberal turn with more private actors such as developers, pension funds and foreign investments funds, and how this is affecting urban development.

This process leaves urban planning with a serious dilemma between the early utopian ideals of the profession and the need to infiltrate and understand the new conditions of the global *polis economicus*. Moreover, it creates new dilemmas regarding the ethics of architecture and the role of the architect and urbanist, when cooperating with and mediating between many stakeholders. The new dilemmas also entail the export of supposedly humanist and democratic Danish welfare architecture to other (perhaps less democratic) parts of the world. Navigating the complexity of the market-driven city is thus the main challenge for urban planning in a world not governed by utopian ideals but by pragmatism and compromise. The current transition from welfare cities to wealth cities is changing the game of urbanism fundamentally. A shift mirroring the transition of the social welfare state towards a market-driven competition state.

In just three decades, the basic myth of the city as an all-inclusive space, where people of different social classes could meet and make a living side by side, has been challenged. From inclusive, information-rich cities with an abundance of culture and economic networks to tap into, we are moving towards increasingly information-poor cities, exporting low-income citizens to the periphery. In turn, the process of deindustrialization and deruralization of the province, and a move towards more knowledge-based workplaces located in the bigger cities, produces an uneven development within the different parts of Denmark. Urbanism used to be about the manipulation of urban space, promoting a lifestyle of the contemporary. Now it is about minimizing the effects of the economic inequalities of the masses, e.g. the 'Ghetto Package' adopted by the Danish parliament of 2018 in order to change the development of socially deprived New Towns from the post-war period, or various efforts aiming to 'revitalize' or 'rebrand' the shrinking cities and the depopulating countryside. Thus, a massive transition of the European cities on a structural, economic and political level is evident. Ideals of the good life and the common good are renegotiated as the urban demographics and culture are changing and society is diversifying with new family patterns and more citizens of non-Danish origin.

In the book Konkurrencestaten (The *Competition State*), published in 2011, the political scientist Ove Kaj Pedersen used the concept of 'competition state' to describe the changes of the welfare state. A concept introduced in the mid-1990s by Philip Cerny.

'*The social state* that introduced state funding in the late 1800s for illness, disability and old age.

The welfare society, which from the 1950s onwards linked prosperity to welfare and welfare to democratization but also to the right to social benefits, the duty of self-sufficiency and finally voluntary participation in co-responsibility for the welfare of others. Thus, state funding was extended to include voluntary participation.

The welfare state, which from the 1970s extended state funding with state control and governance of businesses and households and created welfare policies aimed at promoting full employment but also an expansive system of institutions to increase labour supply.

The competition state, which from the 1990s onwards introduced state control of the public sector, established incentive management of citizens, linked payment of social benefits with connection with the labour market and invested in general in preventing unemployment with the aim of limiting the public sector's costs but also to increase the flexibility of the labor market.'

(Ove K. Pedersen and *Mandag Morgen* in 'Ove K. Pedersen, 'Der er håb for konkurrencestaten', *Information*, 2018)

Snapshot by Jan Gehl diagnosing the present state of Copenhagen. (Jan Gehl)

The central urban square Israels Plads by SWECO and Cobe, which attracts many children with skateboards and BMXs, opened to the public in 2014. (Per Andersen/KADK DOCS)

The recent grooming and social ascent of the Danish capital is an ambivalent phenomenon. As the urban planner and critic Peter Schultz Jørgensen writes, Copenhagen's evolution over the past couple of decades might be international front page news with its bikes, harbour baths, café culture, new public spaces and other popular amenities, but an urban development such as this that rhymes with branding-friendly liveability also comes with a price: a certain degree of social exclusion and what he calls 'social filtering'.

'Indisputably, Copenhagen has become a better place to live, be and get around in than it was 20 years ago. But underneath the roll turf, the pop-up beach and the roots of the roof gardens, there are powerful undercurrents driven by ideologies of the competition state and the competition municipality and financialized real-estate and credit markets. Leading up to this was the neoliberal turn in Copenhagen. In 1990, the conservative prime minister, Poul Schlüter, declared that the capital needed to "take up the competition with other cities in Western Europe." This statement represented a stop to the welfare state, which was to be slimmed down and rolled back rather than developed and refined. Concepts such as inter-urban competition, locomotive and metropolis described the main perspective for Copenhagen. Today, the same view is expressed more delicately in the municipal plan: "Copenhagen's 'liveability' is a strong suit in the international competition", with social filtering as a side effect. The city's soft image is monetized. In the view from the Social Democratic Lord Mayor's windows, Copenhagen has become a city without shadows.'

(Peter Schultz Jørgensen, 'City Without Shadows' in *Critical City*. Copenhagen: The Danish Architectural Press, 2019, pp. 51-53)

Cykelslangen (The Bicycle Snake) by Dissing + Weitling (2014) is an elevated, meandering bicycle bridge, conveniently connecting Vesterbro and Islands Brygge for around 20,000 bicycle commuters a day. Being a bicycle-friendly city is part of Copenhagen's sustainable and liveable image, which attracts many tourists willing to try for themselves. (Per Andersen/KADK DOCS)

Much of the architecture in the new neighbourhoods of Copenhagen is quite generic. (Cecilie Nellemann)

The ten most liveable cities

Country	City	Rank	Overall Rating (100=ideal)	Stability	Healthcare	Culture & Environment	Education	Infrastructure
Austria	Vienna	1	99.1	100	100	96.3	100	100
Australia	Melbourne	2	98.4	95	100	98.6	100	100
Australia	Sydney	3	98.1	95	100	97.2	100	100
Japan	Osaka	4	97.7	100	100	93.5	100	96.4
Canada	Calgary	5	97.5	100	100	90	100	100
Canada	Vancouver	6	97.3	95	100	100	100	92.9
Canada	Toronto	7	97.2	100	100	97.2	100	89.3
Japan	Tokyo	7	97.2	100	100	94.4	100	92.9
Denmark	Copenhagen	9	96.8	95	95.8	95.4	100	100
Australia	Adelaide	10	96.6	95	100	94.2	100	96.4

Liveability has become a mantra in the interurban competition of recent times. The City of Copenhagen operates with a liveability index similar to the Global Liveability Index, presented here by *The Economist.* In line with the new public management and evaluation culture of the past two or three decades, various rating systems are faithfully monitored and employed by the City of Copenhagen to inform their urban development strategies. As the welfare state is moving more in the direction of what the political scientist Ove Kaj Pedersen has called the 'competition state', cities are competing about being voted the happiest, greenest, safest, smartest etc. – and hence the most attractive to investors, good taxpayers and tourists – city in the world. How does this correlate with former ambitions of planning for 'the common good' and 'the good life' of the citizens? (Graphic quoted from website of the The Economist www.economist.com accessed 14 February 2020)

'Mixed housing', 'mixed neighbourhoods' and 'mixed cities' have become key concepts in the present-day situation characterized by increasing inequality and segregation, GhettoPlans and a lack of social cohesion. Three high-profile Social Democrats, Lord Mayor Frank Jensen, Prime Minister Mette Frederiksen and Minister of the resurrected Housing Ministry, Kaare Dybvad, are posing to advocate for the good cause. Few can afford to live on the address Gammel Strand in Copenhagen's old city centre where the campaign poster was hanging in January 2020. Affordable housing is a rare commodity in the Danish capital. (Signe Sophie Bøggild)

Tabel 1. Liste over ghettoområder pr. 1. december 2019

Område		Kommune	Beboere (1.000 +) 1. jan 2019	Udenfor arb.marked > 40 pct. 2017-18	E & I Ikke vestlig > 50 pct. 1. jan 2019	Dømte ≥ 2,03 pct. 2017-18	Kun grundskole > 60 pct. 1. jan 2019	Gns. indkomst < 55 pct. År 2018
Lundtoftegade		København	1.532	32,8	55,4	3,05	60,4	55,0
Aldersrogade		København	2.193	33,3	70,9	1,65	64,4	52,8
Mjølnerparken		København	1.659	38,0	80,5	2,02	75,2	49,6
Tingbjerg/Utterslevhuse		København	6.626	25,7	73,0	2,04	75,4	52,8
Bispeparken		København	1.558	30,9	57,9	3,13	60,4	56,2
Hørgården		København	1.583	32,4	52,1	2,32	61,8	57,9
Tåstrupgård		Høje-Taastrup	2.181	27,0	65,1	1,88	83,0	52,5
Gadehavegård		Høje-Taastrup	2.189	36,2	56,4	2,07	71,8	55,2
Nøjsomhed/Sydvej		Helsingør	1.084	41,1	54,6	2,27	72,7	51,7
Karlemoseparken	ny	Køge	1.452	38,3	51,0	2,09	64,1	64,2
Agervang		Holbæk	1.414	41,7	56,2	1,38	67,4	61,7
Ringparken, Slagelse		Slagelse	2.008	41,2	57,0	2,07	70,2	57,7
Motalavej		Slagelse	1.674	38,6	51,7	2,20	72,1	60,1
Lindholm		Guldborgsund	1.527	48,7	51,6	1,22	64,6	55,6
Solbakken mv		Odense	1.331	41,5	53,0	2,55	62,4	56,0
Korsløkkeparken Øst		Odense	2.066	45,2	62,1	1,63	65,4	61,5
Vollsmose		Odense	7.767	49,5	76,6	2,70	77,2	53,3
Nørager/Søstjernevej m.fl		Sønderborg	1.327	44,7	67,0	1,81	75,6	60,9
Stengårdsvej		Esbjerg	1.342	43,6	79,0	2,69	84,1	55,9
Korskærparken	ny	Fredericia	1.962	40,1	50,1	1,85	68,8	63,2
Sundparken		Horsens	1.588	47,8	69,1	1,21	78,4	54,7
Munkebo		Kolding	1.465	40,5	61,7	1,59	72,2	65,5
Skovvejen/Skovparken		Kolding	2.324	39.8	65,9	2,35	72,7	59,4
Finlandsparken		Vejle	1.586	41,1	74,0	1,03	77,2	62,7
Resedavej/Nørrevang II		Silkeborg	1.876	41,4	52,1	1,82	67,4	61,3
Bispehaven		Aarhus	2.237	43,9	67,5	1,96	71,9	56,8
Skovgårdsparken		Aarhus	1.476	39,6	70,5	2,14	65,6	59,9
Gellerupparken/Toveshøj		Aarhus	5.191	49,3	80,8	2,96	82,0	53,9

Kilde: Trafik-, Bygge- og Boligstyrelsen baseret på udtræk fra Danmarks Statistiks forskerordning.
Anm.: Afrunding har ikke betydning for, om et boligområde opfylder kriteriet for andel dømte og værdierne er derfor vist med det antal decimaler, der er nødvendige for at se, om et område lever op til kriteriet. Der er i december 2019, brugt en anden beregningsmetode for opgørelsen af beboersammensætningen i de 15 *hårde ghettoområder*. Ghettokriterierne for de 15 hårde ghettoområder er beregnet på baggrund af beboere i samtlige boliger i området (herunder familieboliger, ældreboliger og ungdomsboliger). Den nye beregningsmetode har kun marginal betydning i 2019, men vil få stor betydning i takt med, at udviklingsplanerne for de hårde ghettoområder implementeres.

Since 2010, the Danish government has published an annual 'ghetto list', listing the socially deprived neighbourhoods in need of a particular effort. Some areas top the list each year, while others appear on and off, since it is a question of numbers and margins. The parameters determining whether a neighbourhood is to be considered a ghetto are five-fold: 50% or more of residents are immigrants or descendants of people with non-Western background, overall level of income compared to households outside the area, overall educational level, criminal records and unemployment rates. In areas defined as 'hard ghettos' the police is given mandate to temporarily implement zones of exception, where certain kinds of criminal behaviour are punished with double sentences. (Graphic quoted from the website DanmarkC TV https://www.danmarkc.tv/korskaerparken-er-tilbage-paa-ghettolisten/ accessed 25 May 2020)

In 2018, a majority of the Danish parliament voted for the so-called 'parallel society package' or 'Ghetto Package' in order to regenerate and 'normalize' disadvantaged social housing estates with 1,000 residents or more. In the report *Ét Danmark uden parallelsamfund* (*One Denmark without Parallel Societies*), political strategies aiming to eliminate so-called ghettos once and for all are outlined. Socially deprived neighbourhoods are designated as 'parallel societies' – enclaves outside of the 'normal society'. Since the publication of the report, the meaning and definition of the new concept of 'parallel society' was discussed vis-à-vis the relationship between the majority and minorities of the population and social cohesion. The report announced a number of transformations, including the physical environment, of these housing estates.

'The government wishes for a cohesive Denmark. A Denmark built on democratic values such as freedom and rule of law. Equal worth and open-mindedness. Tolerance and gender equality. A Denmark where everybody participates actively.

Over the past 40 years, Denmark's ethnic composition has changed significantly. Parallel societies have developed amongst people of non-Western backgrounds.

The government wishes to prevent and demolish parallel societies. We want to put a stop to the development where those who live in parallel societies do not meet the common Denmark. And where we in some places witness a behaviour conflicting with the rights, obligations and democratic, liberal values of freedom upon which our society is built.

We set forth an ambitious goal that there shall be no ghettos in Denmark by 2030. All ghettos must go. All.

It requires a massive effort to reconvert the vulnerable housing areas into ordinary districts. Among others, by selling existing buildings and making strategic demolitions. And by constructing new privately owned homes.

We release the money needed to complete the task via the fund of the social housing sector (Landsbyggefonden). In total 12 billion Danish kroner for the vulnerable housing areas until 2026. We make clear demands to the social housing sector and the municipalities. If against expectations they shall not be able to meet the task, the state will take over.'

(The Government, the Ministry of the Economy and Interior, *Ét Danmark uden parallelsamfund – ingen ghettoer i 2030*. March, 2018)

SOCIAL HOUSING RESISTANCE

As a reaction against the Government's Ghetto Package, residents in ghetto-labelled social housing estates formed an association called Almen Modstand (Social Housing Resistance). This is their mission statement:

'We are a group of residents from different parts of the social housing sector that have started the initiative Almen Modstand. We are a non-parliamentarian and party-politically neutral platform anchored in the local housing areas.

We have come into being as a reaction to the government's legislative package "One Denmark without parallel societies – no ghettos by 2030". We have decided to funnel our frustration into organizing ourselves with the hope of creating popular resistance against the political legislative proposals that, if the government has it their way, will soon change our rights and our housing areas significantly.

Simultaneously, this is a spontaneous proclamation saying that we can no longer accept the politicians' ghetto-paradigm, which we believe stigmatizes us on the background of categories such as educational and income levels as well as stereotypical imaginaries around ethnicity and nationality. We find that it is absolutely outrageous to discriminate a country's citizens and create unequal rights in this manner.'

(Website of Almen Modstand: http://almenmodstand.dk/hvem/ accessed 6 March 2020)

STIGMATIZATION, JUST DON'T SAY IT OUT LOUD

Shortly after becoming minister of the revived Ministry of Housing, founded in 1947 and shelved 2001-2019, the Social Democrat Kaare

Dybvad, who is also a geographer and author of books on urban development and social inequality, announced that he doesn't want to label social housing estates as ghettos – something he sees as a stigma. Nevertheless, he declared that he was still supporting the overall content of the ghetto law of 2018.

> '— As a minister, some of the first I will do is to stop using ghetto as a concept, he tells *Politiken*.
>
> — When you have been out there and seen people fight to make ends meet, it is very clear that it affects them using the negative expression. And as a minister I will not judge them, he says.
>
> Meanwhile, the minister of housing also emphasizes that he stands by the entire legislative package of so-called ghetto laws that was enacted by parliament last year.
>
> In it the word ghetto appears multiple times and the ghettos are divided into categories of hard ghettos, ghetto areas and vulnerable housing areas.'
>
> (Kaare Dybvad quoted in Ritzau, 'Ny boligminister vil undgå ordet ghetto': https://www.dr.dk/nyheder/politik/ny-boligminister-vil-undga-ordet-ghetto accessed 26 May 2020)

SOCIAL ENGINEERING

In this comment, the urban researcher and professor emeritus Hans Skifter Andersen warns that the Ghetto Package risks repeating the failed social engineering of the past. According to Skifter Andersen, demolition of housing blocks and eviction of locals are not effective means when it comes to solving the problem of segregation.

> 'There have always been social problems in the city districts where the majority for various reasons does not wish to live, and therefore this is why there is space for the socially weaker who do not have a selection of choices on the housing market.
>
> The bombastic and extremely expensive measures of the ghetto-package cannot avoid the elimination of social housing units as a consequence. In the best case scenario the measures will relocate the problems to other districts in the city, in the worst case they will lead to homelessness and an export of the socially vulnerable

residents to the peripheral regions.

Experiences from the Dutch demolitions show that segregation has not been reduced as the residents have merely been relocated to other vulnerable housing areas. If even just a fraction of the billions of DKK that are now being extracted from the residents' collective savings in Landsbyggefonden were invested in already ongoing initiatives in the socially disadvantaged areas, a great deal could be achieved.'

(Hans Skifter Andersen, 'Nedrivning af almene boliger vil ikke mindske segregationen', comment in *Information*, 22 November 2018)

HOMELESSNESS – AN EXTREME KIND OF VULNERABILITY

While social housing units are being selected for demolition, new neighbourhoods with large and expensive flats for upper-middle-class income groups are being developed, and the Danish liveability brand successfully travels the world, the welfare city has simultaneously experienced an increase in citizens without a home. A complex problem which is critically addressed by the publicly funded Council for the Socially Marginalized.

'A dwelling is just as basic a requirement as food and clothing and provides the base from which a person can unfold his/her life. To be without a home can therefore be deeply problematic and it can worsen both social and health-related problems, as well as the person's possibilities to contribute to the community.

In 2009, there were 4,998 homeless people in Denmark. In the latest count of homeless people from 2019 (VIVE makes a count every second year in week 6), the number had risen to 6,431.

(...)

There is a general lack of affordable housing (3,000 – 4,000 DKK/month) in Denmark and particularly in the larger cities. (...) Yet for many years the municipalities have not been capable of building a sufficient number of affordable homes.

(...)

The council believes that fighting homelessness should be top of the political agenda. It simply is a declaration of bankruptcy that homelessness exists in a welfare society such as the Danish. The equality gap between a homeless citizen and other Danes is massive.'

(Website of The Council for The Socially Marginalized: https://www.udsatte.dk/indsatsomrader/hjemloeshed/, accessed 10 March 2020)

RESIDENTS OF MJØLNERPARKEN TAKE THE STATE TO COURT

On 27 May 2020, residents of the social housing estate Mjølnerparken, labelled as 'hard ghetto' and thus subject to transformations including the selling off of rental flats, filed a suit against the state. They are considering it as discriminating being forced to move from their homes simply because of their non-Western origin. The number of residents with non-Western background is enough for a social housing estate to be categorized as a ghetto in need of integration and transformation.

'Kirsten Ketscher, a professor at the University of Copenhagen specializing in non-discrimination and equality law, is surprised that the legislative package enacted by the previous government with support from S, SF and DF wasn't halted by the Justice Department already in 2018.

"The legality of these massive interventions should have been brought forth and debated with more thoroughness. If the residents win the case, and there are good possibilities for that, it will be necessary to reevaluate a range of other laws that are based on ethnicity too," she says.

(...) Asif Mehmood and his wife have raised three girls in Mjølnerparken who have all completed or are enrolled in higher education. "I have always felt accepted by the Danish society. But why must I be kicked out of my flat that doesn't cost more than for me to be able to cover all expenses? It isn't a Danish value to side-step the rights of the citizens because of their income or ethnicity," he says.'

(Frank Hvilsom, 'Mjølnerparken hiver staten i retten for diskrimination', *Politiken*, 27 May 2020)

Which role can cultural heritage and listing potentially play in the evaluation of the post-war welfare city? Art historians and researchers Svava Riesto and Rikke Stenbro examine which dwellings built after 1945 have been listed, where they are located, and who lives in them. While the law says that listings should represent the living conditions of the population, Riesto and Stenbro's analysis demonstrate that the listed buildings are predominantly villas by famous architects like Jørn Utzon and Arne Jacobsen, inhabited by a privileged social group. Why is that? Perhaps it is time to start a broader societal discussion of cultural heritage, listing and the values underpinning preservation, urban transformation, gentrification and demolitions of homes?

'In periods of high building activity, there tends to be an increased interest in preserving historical monuments, built environments and cultural landscapes. During the building boom of the 1960s and 1970s, when the Danish landscapes and cities changed like never before, preservation became an increasingly important topic in society.

There was a growing interest in the general living conditions of the population, both in new architecture and historical preservation in those years. In effect, from the 1970s onwards some historical homes of ordinary, and even poor people, in many different parts of the country were designated with the highest national protection, listing.[1]

Today, when the urban environment is once again facing massive changes, there is a renewed interest in preservation among local residents and activists. Yet, according to a new survey of listed post-war housing,[2] the interest in the living conditions of the general public that was raised in the 1960s and 1970s is not reflected in contemporary listing practice. (...)

(...) Housing from the 1960s and 1970s plays a significant role in the individual and collective experiences and memories of people in Denmark and the history of society. These buildings are situated throughout all of Denmark, in big cities, smaller towns and in the countryside. The many new homes were divided among two types: standardized single-family detached houses, which were privately owned, and large-scale social housing.[3] Both types were subsidized by the state.

(...)

Today, these buildings and landscapes have become historical and they face multiple changes, such as decay, renovation, renewal, climate adaptation, densification and demolition projects. These changes are related to socio-political changes, gentrification, new standards for living conditions, new political agendas and new ideas about quality of life, urbanism, etc., and require a reevaluation of the significance and values of this legacy in the present for the future. The question is, how are the massive efforts of the Danish welfare state, which has had and still has a major impact on people's living conditions and is a significant part of the societal history, represented in contemporary architecture preservation? More specifically, how does the state practice of listing buildings address housing that was built from 1945 up to the present?

WHAT IS LISTED (AND WHAT IS NOT)?

In recent decades several initiatives have been made in order to protect buildings, built environments and landscapes from the period after 1945. A committee dedicated specifically to the protection of post-1940 architecture was established under the preservation NGO *Landsforeningen for By- og Landskabskultur*[5] in 2012. The national preservation agency Slots- og Kulturstyrelsen,[6] which has the regulatory responsibility for sites, monuments and listed buildings, supported the new committee. The agency announced that they see it as "essential that in the years ahead there is focus on the protection of this enormous and important stock of buildings [from the postwar period], which has had a major influence on the lives of all Danes." [7]

When examining which buildings dating from the post-war era that have been selected for listing and which have not, it is striking that the most preferred types of housing that accommodated the most people and which were erected in large numbers throughout the country, remain absent from the list today. Neither social housing estates, where one out of five people in Denmark live,[8] nor mass-produced single-family housing – of which there is more than one million in Denmark[9] – are represented through listing. This is striking considering that the purpose of listing, as stated by The Danish Building

Preservation Act, is to "*safeguard old buildings that reflect essential features of societal development* [....] *including housing conditions.*" (...)

(...)

From the 1960s and onwards, the usual perspective of history that had focused on royalty, heads of state and other people in power, has been criticized and the political implications of history addressed. There has been a growing acknowledgement that history can be viewed from multiple perspectives and new historical enquiries into woman's history, children's history, microhistory, the history of minorities, etc. In line with this expanded notion of history, national heritage in Denmark began to include the living conditions of previously underrepresented groups in listing, especially since the 1970s. From this perspective, it is ironic that when listing housing from this same period, the state reproduces histories with an anteceded singularity and a power perspective that has been under critique for more than half a century. (...)

THE ROLE OF LISTING IN SOCIETY AND FUTURE PERSPECTIVES

(...) We call for a public discussion about the purpose of listing and its role in society, if indeed it is still relevant at all. Observing the rise of activism in Denmark in recent years, when new groups of citizens and young people have engaged in protests about the protection of buildings as well as nature conservation, it becomes clear that preservation concerns more than the representation of an architectural canon.[10] This suggests that listing can be mobilized as a resistance to short-term planning that can work against gentrification and the exploitation of shared resources. As a historical practice, listing buildings can create a more inclusive understanding of the past that represents and gives voice to multiple previously underrepresented groups.

In any case, to remain relevant in a democratic welfare society, listing must become a self-reflexive and transparent practice whose values and political implications are openly discussed.'

[1]

E.g. Poorhouse (*fattiggård*) in Sønderho, Fanø from 1840 (listed i 1971); Worker's housing, Overgaden oven Vande, built by Aktieselskabet til oprettelse af boliger for Arbejderklassen in 1851 (listed in 1981), Gyngehuset Landarbejderhus in Faaborg Midtfyn municipality built 1852, (listed i 1994). See also Jannie Rosenberg Bendsen og Mogens A. Morgen, *Fredet – Bygningsfredning i Danmark 1918-2018*, Copenhagen: Strandberg Publishing 2018.

[2]

The full survey is published in: Svava Riesto & Rikke Stenbro (2019), 'Mesterværkerne, eliten og dem, der var flest af: Værdiopfattelser og blinde vinkler i fredningen af velfærdssamfundets boliger'. *Fabrik og Bolig*, (1), 32-48. This article also presents a more comprehensive analysis of our findings and puts them into context.

[3]

The Danish term *almene boliger* (previously *Almennyttige boliger*) is difficult to translate into English. Some chose to translate it as public housing, since this form of housing is not restricted to those with the greatest need, but a comprehensive, state-funded sector of rental housing. We chose the translation social housing here, since this is how the sector presents itself in English, see e.g. Natalia Anna Rogaczewska et al. (ed.), *How to House*, Copenhagen: BL Danmarks almene boliger 2015.

[5]

National Association for Building and Landscape Culture.

[6]

The English name is: The Danish Agency for Culture and Palaces.

[7]

https://us1.campaign-archive.com/?u=47db7cc4a4786fd0a0f601187&id=32bfdbe044&e=093e861db3

[8]

Natalia Anna Rogaczewska et al. (ed.), *How to House*, Copenhagen: BL Danmarks almene boliger 2015.

[9]

According to Statistics Denmark, there is today more than 1,100,000 inhabited standardized single-family housing 'parcelhus-stuehuse' in Denmark http://curis.ku.dk/

[10]

Examples of this are the protests against development in the green areas of Amager Fælled and Stejlepladsen in Copenhagen, and the protests against the demolition of Slagtergårdene in the Vesterbro district, in which listing was an explicit theme. Also, the activist group Almen Modstand, which formed in response to the state 'Ghetto Plan', can be understood as a movement in favour of the preservation of social housing, although in another sense than traditional listing.

(Abbreviated version of the article Svava Riesto & Rikke Stenbro, 'Mesterværkerne, eliten og dem, der var flest af: Værdiopfattelser og blinde vinkler i fredningen af velfærdssamfundets boliger', in *Fabrik og Bolig* (1), 2019, pp. 32-48)

Views on *whose* history it is important to tell have been challenged and expanded over the last fifty years. In 1974, Vejle Kunstmuseum held an exhibition titled *Everyday Pictures*, in which selected artists as well as the construction workers who had worked on renovating the museum were invited to contribute their everyday pictures for the show. The artist collective Røde Mor conceived several posters for the exhibition. (Illustration used with permission from Thomas Kruse)

kilde: Danmarks Statistik

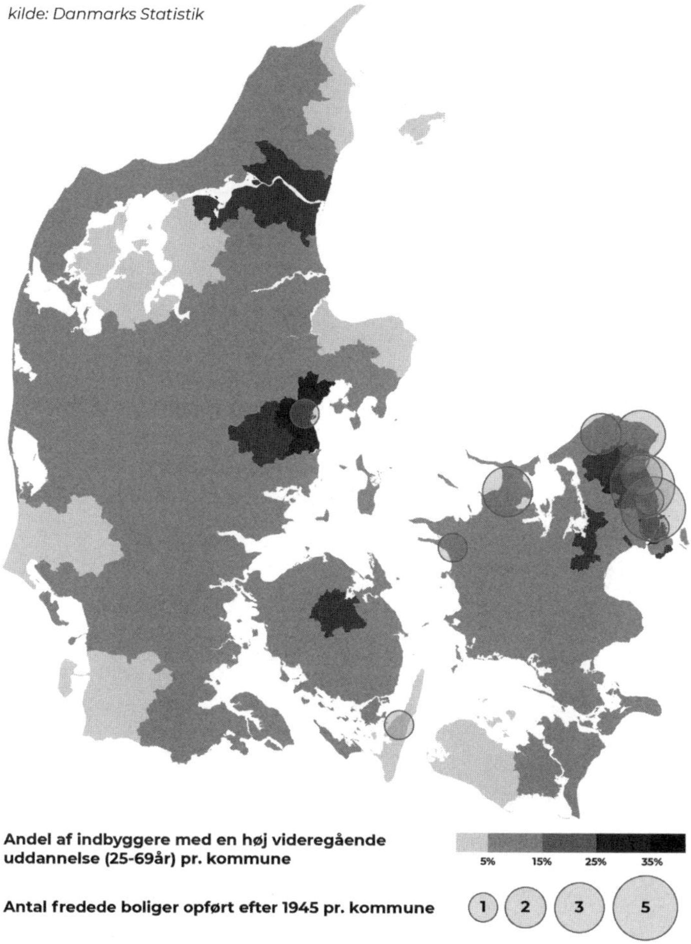

The selection of listed residences from the post-war period has a significant geographic predominance from North Zealand. A comparison between this selection and a map showing the population's educational levels reveals that, at present, listed residences from the period after 1945 are only found in places where the most educated and financially affluent live; that is, in the few municipalities in which more than 35% of all residents between the ages of 25 and 69 have studied at postgraduate level. (Graphic illustration by Jovana Pavic, Rikke Stenbro and Svava Riesto, based on information obtained from the list of buildings designated as worthy of preservation, as well as Statistics Denmark. First published in *Fabrik & Bolig* 2019)

Scene from a protest against the demolition of occupied flats in Gellerupparken, a welfare housing estate near Aarhus dating from the 1960s. This is one of many demonstrations against the law popularly referred to as *Ghettopakken*, which leads to privatization and/or demolition of social housing estates in Denmark. Although not associated with the official heritage sector and historic preservation organizations, these protests do promote the preservation of post-war housing and show that discussions about preservation are neither innocent nor self-evident but are tied to political agendas. (Photo by Bo Sigismund)

WITH, FOR OR AGAINST ALL? PROFIT AND PUBLIC INTEREST IN SCANDINAVIAN LARGE-SCALE HOUSING ESTATES

In this abbreviated article, architect and researcher Heidi Svenningsen Kajita discusses the interests – including economic and demographic – involved in the transformation of socially deprived housing estates. Interviewing locals about diversity work and everyday life, she compares the situation in Denmark and Sweden.

"“When it was owned by MKB, the municipal housing association, we had eleven rooms spread out over Lindängen [and] loads of activities; table tennis, billiards, a photography club, joinery, youth workshop, model railway, a fishing club ... It was the sort of thing that we should have available for the young people today [...] MKB sold Lindängen in 1987. That was when all the hobby activities stopped. [They] sold Lindängen to a company. Then, that company went bankrupt. It was Stadshypotek and Stenafinans. To make their money back, they split the flats between them [...] Stadshypotek sold theirs later to, among others, a Danish property investor. He bought that whole part for 317 million [SEK] and then, half a year later, sold it for 434 million [SEK]. So that was a good profit. Then it was sold again, and once again."[1]

The Nordic model is renowned for its decency and collectivist mindset in support of fundamental needs such as non-profit housing for all. But recent decades' globalized economies and migration patterns can be seen to challenge this approach. During the post WW2 era the Swedish and Danish Welfare States orchestrated large-scale housing estates as part of a greater universal housing system to meet both economic growth and social needs. Building construction was industrialized and rationalized during this period, and companies established then have since prospered into globalized businesses. However, the social ideals of this post-war housing staled. MR M, quoted above, is a long-term resident in Lindängen on the outskirts of Malmö – one of the so-called *Million Programme* housing estates. He describes how profit speculation over the years has come to work against the estate's community spaces. First imagined for the social good of all, the estates are increasingly reported as cause of segregation.

There is broad agreement across different stakeholders that diversity work is needed in the organization of the social and housing: new infrastructural links; new housing typologies etc. are seen to connect and mix the estates with the surrounding cities. It is however less obvious how such physical diversification addresses the troublesome needs arising from increasing inequalities at the heart of segregation issues. To question these relationships, I look to Sarah Ahmed's reanimation of diversity work. In a study of universities, she queers and skews the terms use and utilitarianism to provoke inclusivity that "build from the needs of those who are not enabled by following [well-used] routes."[2] Ahmed introduces the notion of "queer use" understood as something used by someone for whom it was not intended. So, what is the use of non-profit housing?

In Sweden a spiral of stigma, deregulation and privatization has contributed to dismantling the once idealized housing estates and welfare for all.[3] But recent scholarship has revealed how private investors again today re-invest in the social potential offered by the planning of this multi-family housing. After decades of deregulating the socio-economic ties of housing, concepts such as long-term affordability, sustainability and social capital are made popular in dialogues with both municipalities and residents. However, private companies may limit access to their housing on terms of tenants' income, employment etc.[4] The new notions of welfare, this time for-profit, are not for all. In the Danish context, the nationwide organization of the non-profit housing sector has historically worked for universalist ends that are now challenged by anti-segregation strategies such as the action plan "A Denmark without Parallel Societies – No Ghettos in 2030."[5] Based on "a relatively simple causal model," this plan "emphasizes that immigration coupled with insufficient sanctions and requirements have led immigrants to 'lump together'."[6] The basic solution is to target specific non-profit housing areas marked as "hard ghettos" and here to reduce the number of family units to a maximum of 40% before 2030 by densifying, selling off to private investors, demolishing or re-categorizing units e.g. as student housing. But the build environment is managed in tandem with punitive policies, including mandatory childcare and criminalization of 're-education trips', targeting specific residents.[7] The idea is "not [to] trouble all Danes throughout all Denmark".[8] As it happens public interest is turned against the notion of all.

On the ground, profitability and public interest that during the postwar era were envisioned *for* the good of all are today (also) working *against* all. Instead, I plea that architecture and planning communities rethink the social – *with* all. This is not a call for a nostalgic return to modernist universalism and its' promises of trouble-free, good cities and citizens. But from the notion of all, we might bring with us the need for positioning. The non-profit housing sector, and more specifically the large-scale housing estates are affected by neoliberal and cultural assimilation agendas, practices and policies. Here, technologies of architecture and planning are instrumentally used to implement social change that marginalize certain communities. Following Ahmed's thinking, the role assigned to architects' and planners' can be an opening to do diversity work: to rethink agendas already given, re-write briefs already written or re-imagine representative forms already imagined. Ahmed writes: "for a past use not to be exhaustive we have work to do, the work of enabling a tool to be used for other purposes."[9] In architecture and planning such a *What if?* is an expertise already in place. The urban forms of postwar mass-housing have often been causally linked to social problems. But this urban form is also already flexible and has been skewed over time. This form loosely fits neoliberal profit speculation, for-profit- and nonprofit affordable housing and residents' own reproductions of space. There are choices to be made. I urge the architectural and planning communities to dare engage in diversity work with all.'

[1]

Interview with resident in Lindängen on the outskirts of Malmö published in H. Svenningsen Kajita (2016), *Fragile Potentials in the Big Plans – Spatial and material dimensions of Post WW2 large-scale housing in use*, the Royal Danish Academy of Fine Arts, Schools of Architecture, Design and Conservation, Chapter 9 (PhD Dissertation). 'MKB' refers to the municipal housing association MKB Fastighets AB.

[2]

Sarah Ahmed (2019), *What's the use? On the Uses of Use*, Duke University Press, pp. 221-222.

[3]

G. Baeten, S. Westin, E. Pull & I. Molina (2017), 'Pressure and violence: Housing renovation and displacement in Sweden' in *Environment and Planning A: Economy and Space*, 49 (3), pp. 631-651.[4]

S. Westerdahl (2018), 'Against the stream: How a small company builds affordable housing' in *Affordable Housing Governance and Finance: Innovations, partnerships and comparative perspectives*. Ed. Gerard Van Bortel, Vincent Gruis, Joost Nieuwenhuijzen, Ben Pluijmers. Pp 105-122.

[4]

Westerdahl, S. (2018): 'Against the stream: How a small company builds affordable housing' in *Affordable Housing Governance and Finance: Innovations, partnerships and comparative perspectives*. Ed. Gerard Van Bortel, Vincent Gruis, Joost Nieuwenhuijzen, Ben Pluijmers. Pp 105-122.

[5]

Et Danmark uden parallelsamfund. Ingen ghettoer i 2030 (2018) (Eng. *One Denmark without Parallel Societies: No Ghettos in 2030*, author's translation). Danish Government.

[6]

A. Staver, J. Brekke & S. Søholt (2019), *Scandinavia's segregated cities – policies, strategies and ideals*. Norwegian Institute for Urban and Regional Research, Oslo Metropolitan University, p. 7.

[7]

See: DK Prime Ministers' New Years Address 2018. Source: The prime minister's office. http://stm.dk/_p_14611.html. Last accessed February 2020.

[8]

Ibid.

[9]

Ahmed, op. cit., p. 222.

(This text is abbreviated from Heidi Svenningsen Kajita, 'With, For or Against All? Profit and Public Interest in Scandinavian Large-Scale Housing Estates'. In *P.E.A.R.: Paper for Emerging Architectural Research*, Issue VIII. 2021)

TRANSFORMING GELLERUP – FROM NEW TOWN TO AN AARHUS NEIGHBOURHOOD

The New Town Gellerupparken in Aarhus is in many ways a guinea pig for the transformation initiatives and diversity work on social housing estates that emerged in the wake of the 'Ghetto Package'. Thus, Gellerup is about a decade into the process of a total makeover which aims to 'normalize' the district and link it closer to the rest of Aarhus. It is interesting to look at the before and after images of the suburb.

Erected 1968-1972, Gellerupparken in western Aarhus is a New Town designed by Knud Blach Petersen and a clear example of a certain time and ethos when new building materials and systems became means to obtain ambitious goals of mass housing. As a response to housing shortage, quantity was key and defining for the quality. Prefabrication was a prerequisite for economically and technically accomplishing instant housing in mega-scale. Focusing on progress, growth and rationalization, politicians, urban planners and architects shared the view that housing construction should be concentrated in larger units with zoning. As in many other New Towns, the master plan was not realized in its totality, and a section of lower-scale housing was never built. In the beginning, Gellerup was quite exclusive with hotel, tennis court, shopping centre, jazz club, theatre, swimming pool, restaurant etc. The slogan simply read, 'It is good to live in Gellerup!' and in 1980, the techno-pioneers Kraftwerk even gave a concert among the concrete blocks. Gradually, the social status and demography changed from younger pioneer families of Danish origin towards a more ethnic composition with the arrival of guest labourers, refugees and socially disadvantaged Danes referred by the municipality. (Hotel Gellerup brochure and images from Brabrand-Århslev Lokalhistoriske Arkiv)

In the mid-1990s, the developer Olav de Linde invested in a bazaar in Gellerup, based on the idea that it is better for people to run their own business than be placed passively on welfare in order to enforce integration. Thus, residents of the multicultural neighbourhood are selling kebabs, veils and spices to both locals, Aarhusians and even tourists. (Signe Sophie Bøggild)

Renderings of the future upgraded Gellerup, connecting the New Town with the rest of Aarhus. This strategic master plan was agreed upon by the City of Aarhus and the local housing association Brabrand Boligforening as early as 2007. In 2009-2010, the two parties managed compromised on an overall plan which outlined the programme and functions in more detail. The transformative features include new thoroughfares, new path systems, construction of new housing typologies with other ownership-models than social housing, demolitions of existing housing blocks, part of the municipality moving their offices to the area, a new urban park etc. (Courtesy of Transform and Vandkunsten)

In 2019, Aarhus Municipality and Brabrand Boligforening decided to demolish an additional 600 dwellings, in Gellerup and Toveshøj in order to meet the Ghetto Package's demand of having only 40 percent family dwellings of social housing in Denmark's 'hard ghettos' before 2030. Common sense or a new kind of brutalism? Some have called it a "democratic deficit" and there have been local protests. (Aysha Amin)

A CITY PERSPECTIVE – HOW TO MAKE THE CHANGE OF GELLERUP A SUCCESS

Aarhus Municipality explains the mission and vision of the transformation of Gellerup.

'The vision of the master plan (Helhedsplanen) is to create a unique and diverse district with its very own character, architectural expression and city life. A new district uses the existing structures as a point of departure but adds new layers such as neighbourhoods, new housing, road and traffic patterns, buildings, public spaces and green recreational areas.

MISSION

The district is being recreated so that the physical and social isolation of the past will be replaced by diversity in the city life and resident composition. The diversity matches the rest of Aarhus in terms of employment, educational level, income and security.

We create the change together with the residents of the district, the surrounding area and the rest of Aarhus.'

(Website of the master plan for Gellerup and Toveshøj: https://helhedsplangellerup.dk/derfor-goer-vi-det/vision-og-forandringshistorie/ accessed 25 May 2020)

DEFENDING GELLERUP

Managing an architectural studio located in Gellerup's old collective house, which according to the new master plan is ripe for demolition, Anna Mette Exner (daughter of the architect couple Inger and Johannes Exner, who designed brutalist inspired buildings like the Gug and Islev churches) defends the qualities of the existing structures in the Aarhus suburb. For her, it is all about the narrative.

'It is an amazing architecture, it's just in bad repair. Of course, it looks awful right now. It's the responsibility of the politicians – they hate these buildings, and they simply want to demolish them. The worse it comes to look, the better for them. But it's completely derailed to try to transform Gellerup into some sort of average Denmark, Gellerup has a very particular soul.

One of the reasons that Gellerup is problematic right now, is that it is only 50 years old. But by demolishing we are beginning all over; it is a wrong strategy. We should add on, because a city is a living organism that needs to grow quietly.

And we must take off our ghetto-glasses. Since the story about this place is controlled by people from outside, Gellerup is kept in an iron grip. When people visit me here in my studio they start off by saying: "what on earth are you doing in this ugly building?" Then when they go outside and see it and listen to the stories, their attitudes change.'

(Anna Mette Exner quoted in Marie Kraul, 'Aarhus-borgmester i clinch med 175 arkitekter', in *Politiken Byrum* 14 May 2019: https://politikenbyrum.dk/Nyheder/art7194672/%C2%BBJeg-kan-simpelthen-ikke-se-at-der-skulle-v%C3%A6re-specielt-smukt-her-i-Gellerup%C2%AB accessed 11 March 2020)

The book *Helhedsplanen* (The Master Plan) is based on the author Hanne Højgaard Viemose's private experience of living in Gellerup. Among other things, she describes how the current transformations affect everyday life. The efforts include bussing children from Gellerup to other parts of Aarhus as a strategy to enforce the connectivity with the rest of the city.

> 'From my kitchen window, I can see a school and a bus that arrives to transport some of the area's children to other parts of the city so that they won't be negatively influenced by the other kids in the area, it's something Aarhus municipality has decided, they think it's a great idea: to deprive some parents the free choice of school if their children's Danish isn't good enough when they start school, "then it's important that they are taken away from the area burdened by immigrants, ... unfortunately it is our experience that many children are returning to their area when they are given the free choice of school again." (...) "I think ýou can perceive the bus transportation as a resource, for instance, when the children are attending a birthday party in Gellerup, where they are typically from, we can drive them there and back in the bus," says one of the teachers at Holme school to *Jyllands-Posten*. I'm thinking, if perhaps a similar arrangement could be made where the children are screened for self-righteousness, ignorance and hysteria: if, for instance, the children believe that a Filipino is a cleaning machine, sugar and white flour a disease, an iPad a human right, then the parents could be deprived of the free choice of school and the children could be taken by bus to e.g. Trillegården or Gellerupparken, where they could avoid being burdened by children of the same worldview as themselves, yet one must remember to consider the bus transportation as a resource, that they can be taken by bus back and forth.'

(Hanne Højgaard Viemose, *Helhedsplanen*. Aarhus: Små Bjerge i Beton, Jorinde & Joringel, 2016, p. 23)

Young locals have opened the gallery Andromeda8220 in Gellerup. As they write, 'The platform functions as a safe space for expression and exchange of knowledge, made for the empowerment of our community and to connect with the global majority. The intention of having an independent local art platform is to reclaim the agency as inhabitants and individuals in the urban development discussion. Our drive is to empower diversity through art, and to make art accessible with a hands-on and bottom-up way of approach.' (http://andromeda8220.dk/?page_id=16 accessed 4 June 2020) (Andromeda8220)

Hosting many activities, spaces for different uses and collaboration with local associations, Aarhus' new library with citizen service, Dokk1, has been a great success – a kind of 'welfare Versailles': a non-commercial meeting room for all Aarhusians, ranging from groups of students and playing children, over associations meeting and makers trying out new crafts techniques, to foreigners learning about how to become a citizen in Denmark. (Visit Aarhus and Signe Sophie Bøggild)

Now we have looked at Gellerup from urban utopia, over lived reality with certain problems and potentials, to the current transformation according to a new urban imaginary of a mixed and integrated city. Based on the Gellerup case, we might wonder what new New Towns and neighbourhoods can learn from the experiences of the post-war New Towns?

Michelle Provoost, the Dutch architectural historian, director of the International New Town Institute and partner in Crimson Historians and Urbanists, talks about the difference between the New Towns of the post-war period and the 'new' New Towns that are primarily built on other continents such as China, India and in the Gulf states. Moreover, she encourages top-down planning to work together with more bottom-up actors of local citizens.

'The current situation in Western Europe – the crisis of the Euro, the crisis of the financial institutions, the welfare state crisis – leads us to question the relationship between market, state and citizen. As of yet we haven't seen any good answers, and I think that we are in the midst of a phase that will offer some big changes, demanding that we take the citizens very seriously both in politics, city planning and in all parts of society in general.

It starts with the planning. Particularly in the suburbs and in the new, planned cities is it in short supply exactly because they are so well planned on behalf of politicians and planners. It is they who today hold power and competencies that must create the changes necessary for others to be able to join in and contribute to the further development and planning of these areas. It is a very difficult, psychological manoeuvre, and in addition it necessitates that we discard a bunch of regulations, change others and come up with entirely new ones. Designing the organisational structure necessary for it to be possible could very well be the grand planning task of the decade to come.

(...)

What role does the architect play in all of this?

Perhaps it is an idealistic point of view, but if you look at history in the 1950s and 60s, the architects were actually deeply involved in the conceptual development of cities. Not only in the design and construction of icons and public buildings but in designing for the common good and for people's everyday lives. It isn't like that anymore, and the architects have a diminished role and a more superficial role. I don't really see a positive future in that.'

(Jesper Pagh, 'Fra demokratisk velfærdsby til neoliberal utopi', *Arkitekten* 7, 2013, pp. 38-39)

Nordhavn is one the new neighbourhoods in Copenhagen's harbour. Since it includes services, infrastructures and institutions in addition to housing, you can call it a New Town, although it was not built from tabula rasa but rather reuses some of the harbour's old industrial structures. Nordhavn aims to learn from the experience of Ørestad with smaller plots, higher density and more coherence between the individual buildings and the overall plan. The master plan was won by Cobe with Sleth, Polyform and Rambøll, with CPH City & Port Development as a client, in 2008, and the construction is still ongoing. (Rasmus Hjortshøj)

Few have had more influence on Copenhagen's recent development than Jens Kramer Mikkelsen, the former Lord Mayor of Copenhagen and director of CPH City & Port Development. Currently, he works for the private developer NREP, which is involved in the transformation of socially deprived neighbourhoods like Tingbjerg. In this interview, he reflects on the development and the lessons from Ørestad vis-à-vis the next generation New Town of Nordhavn.

'— Nordhavn is the next big project after Ørestad. What have you learned from Ørest...

— You can't say "after Ørestad". It is by far the biggest project today, and it spans so many years into the future. There has been criticism of Ørestad, but urban development is always characterized by the thinking that exists at the time that it is being built. The idea of aesthetics, functionality and economics is evolving, and we can't say 15 years later that it was wrong,' says Jens Kramer Mikkelsen.

"I think those who made decisions on the planning of Ørestad in the 1990s made it based on what was the wisest thinking about *the good city* at that time. We do the same today in Nordhavn. And then of course it may be that the thinking is another in 15 years ...

"The beautifully thought-out city we all like takes many years to build. The 'bridge neighbourhoods', with their audience-oriented offerings on the ground floor, followed by two-three layers of commercial activities and two-three layers of housing on top, were not planned like that to begin with. It is extremely difficult to make, because you rarely have a housing market and a business market that fluctuates at the same time. And who takes the risk and opens a new shop in the living room when there is not a critical mass of people living in the area?"'

(Jens Kramer Mikkelsen, in Jakob Dall, 'Vi skal holde op med at tro, at vi kan få Firenzestemning alle steder i København', *Information*, 20 July 2017)

The model used by CPH City & Port Development: securing funding for Copenhagen's metro through land sale and the construction of numerous dwellings in new neighbourhoods such as Ørestad, Nordhavn and Lynetteholmen, is a debated model. As an alternative strategy, Anne Romme and Morten Birk Jørgensen, both architects and researchers at KADK, Copenhagen's school of architecture, recommend parcelling out building sites into smaller plots. They propose a strategy that could potentially stimulate the construction of a more diverse housing supply, rather than the typical estate agent-friendly solutions. More specifically, Birk Jørgensen and Romme suggest that the debated site of Stejlepladsen in Sydhavnen, where CPH City & Port Development is planning to build after having the area delisted, is transformed into a laboratory of experimental and even self-built housing.

'Copenhagen is expanding like never before. The city has added several major urban areas in recent decades, and 2017 even surpassed the raging urban development of the post-war years in the number of new homes. Today, the islands of Holmen, the expansion of Islands Brygge, Ørestaden, Sydhavnen, large parts of Valby and most recently parts of Nordhavnen have all changed from previous functions such as industrial or military areas to being prominent residential areas. The many new buildings appear to be characterized by a number of common conditions in terms of housing types and building technology, the size and layout of the flats, the surface character and colour of the walls and the nature of the outdoor areas. (...) For the municipality as well as for CPH City & Port Development, business as usual is the convenient and handy option. In this way, the developers develop housing for the largest and strongest group of investors: an upper-middle-class family with a willingness for lifelong indebtedness to get a share of the city's delights. Could you instead imagine that the residents became developers? That the many family types constituting Copenhagen became the main stakeholders as new homes are devised, designed and built? And what does it take for such a scenario to become reality?'

(Anne Romme and Morten Birk Jørgensen, 'Debat: Her er vores tips til By & Havn – lav udstykninger i mindre byggegrunde', *Politiken Byrum*, 31 January 2019)

Similar to the model for Ørestad, the municipality funds a new part of the metro through the sale of plots and development of housing in Nordhavn. (Signe Sophie Bøggild)

Architect Thomas Arnfred, founding partner of Vandkunsten, criticizes the lack of creativity and flexibility in the master plan of Lynetteholmen. The artificial island is to be realized as a New Town for 35,000 residents in the port of Copenhagen by 2070. Seemingly echoing modernist top-down planning, such as Urban Hansen's full-scale Urbanplan from the 1960s and other tabula rasa master plans, Lynetteholmen was presented by the national government and the City of Copenhagen in 2018. Just like a 'Kinder egg', it is supposed to solve Copenhagen's housing shortage and prevent future sea-level rises in one quick fix. In a discussion article, Arnfred, a central figure in the reinvention of Danish housing and new neighbourhoods since the 1970s, criticizes the master plan for its lack of imagination in the approach to urban development on water and the utter absence of poetry or utopian thinking.

'The worst thing, though, is that the illustrations of the prospectus show that there is still a very traditional box and block thinking behind Copenhagen's future development. We cannot allow this. The notion that you can just pour landfill off the quayside when the city needs to grow is obnoxious. Landfill has poor carrying capacity, and pillars must be struck down to a load-bearing chalk layer if the plan's heavy-duty blocks are to be built. But instead of housing blocks one should think alternatively and see the many exciting opportunities that arise when we are out on the water and free of mainland constraints ... Of course, urban development must protect the historic districts against floods, and land is usable for building dikes. Surely, the adapted plan also indicates a scenic transition from city to water, as we know it from Amager Strandpark. Yet, the seabed and the water surface are also a landscape, and parts of the new neighbourhoods behind the dikes may not stand on pillars at all, but flow?

(...)

And now that we know that the capital's future districts must of course be car-free, Lynetteholm's districts must offer a completely different urban space grammar than the one we know from the mainland. I have said this before, but I would like to reiterate: Lynetteholm would thus become the new Venice of the Nordic region with thriving settlements, floating gardens and lovely residential environments. Allow me to claim that it is time for the urban planning people, the architect profession and indeed the entire construction industry, to show us that there are alternatives to the boring template construction of the housing speculation on the mainland.

The climate threat is not only a serious reality but also a great chance to demonstrate that urban planning is intimately linked to thoughtfulness and reason.'

(Jens Thomas Arnfred, 'Det er tarveligt bare at hælde jord ud over kajkanten, når byen skal vokse', discussion article in *Politiken Byrum*, 11 September 2019)

Rendering of Lynetteholmen, the new New Town which is going to be built from scratch on an artificial island in Copenhagen's harbour. (Courtesy of the former Ministry of Transport, Building and Housing)

The urban farm Østergro, which is located in a former car-repair shop on Østerbro in Copenhagen, is an example of local grassroots joining forces to make a new urban space for community and food production. Such bottom-up initiatives might inspire new planning processes and remind us of the value of green spaces in the city. The farm supplies local families with vegetables, teaches Copenhageners how to do organic gardening and includes a roof restaurant. Østergro is a local case of the international urban gardening movement reclaiming public space and green oases, an evidence of the increasing awareness and mobilization of commons and communities. (Courtesy of Østergro)

In this feature article, Ellen Braae, professor of Landscape Architecture and Urbanism at the University of Copenhagen, criticizes the prioritization of recent urban development. While densification has been a mantra for some years, she questions whether this urban strategy truly benefits the cities and citizens. According to her, densification with high-rises in new neighbourhoods like Aarhus Ø and Sydhavnen in Aarhus risks eliminating some of the green lungs in the city, at once decreasing the quality of life for the locals and worsening the situation of the environment. An argument that the Covid-19 pandemic has supported. Thus, Braae requests a more sensitive and strategic city and park politics from Aarhus Municipality. As always, economy plays a major role in prioritizations.

> 'We are increasingly connecting notions of "the good life" with "the good city life". Caffè latte on a sun-drenched urban area stands as the guiding picture. In addition, the city has increasingly become a socio-economic engine in itself, and thus investment goals for developers and the pension funds we are all for better or worse part of ... It is good business to build many square metres of living space on a small plot of land. All of these conditions uncritically pull in the same direction. At the expense of daylight and free space (...) I miss some voices that manage to speak qualitatively about how the city should evolve in favour of "the public good" – sorry for the old-fashioned words. There are currently no visions for how the city's common, green structures should evolve. The current forests and parks cannot handle the pressure of the many, many new users. And it would serve the city well to think about how all these new buildings are affecting the city, and also whether it is again so super-smart to block the link between the city and the sea, as we see on both Aarhus Ø and Sydhavnen?'

(Ellen Braae, 'Aarhus savner en by- og parkpolitik', in *Jyllands-Posten*, April 27 2017)

The height, density and urbanity of Aarhus' new neighbourhood Aarhus Ø on the harbour front have been debated both among professionals and locals. (Signe Sophie Bøggild)

The housing economist Curt Liliegreen, director of The Knowledge Centre for Housing Economics, speaks of an unbalanced Denmark: there is not one but various real estate markets in Denmark. Contrary to 30 years ago when Copenhagen Municipality was on the verge of bankruptcy, the situation has changed significantly. As in other countries, there is a growing pressure on the bigger cities and their nearby suburbs, while more 'peripheral' parts, marked by deindustrialization and brain drain, are lacking behind when it comes to selling housing for profit and attracting 'good taxpayers'.

> 'Denmark does not have only one housing market but several regional markets that operate at different speeds. Moreover, the difference between these markets has increased during the past few years. When considering prices and a property's time on the market, the scattering has increased. The difference between a property's time on the market in the capital versus the provinces has become bigger and bigger.
>
> (...)
>
> It is not a catastrophe, yet it certainly isn't an indicator of overheating either. There have been differences between the regional housing markets before, but these differences have now increased.'

(Curt Liliegreen, 'Husk det nu – Danmark har ikke ét boligmarked', blogpost 6 September 2016 on https://www.bvc.dk/almen-formidling/husk-det-nu-danmark-har-ikke-%C3%A9t-boligmarked accessed 26 May 2020)

The experience economy of big events, festivals and tourism is an important part of the story about how the city is sold and told. Urban spaces are staged as fancy backdrops attracting the attention of investors and the public. One example is the annual Copenhagen Marathon – one of many sports events that have become part of the collective dream – or nightmare – of the Copenhageners. Another case is the publicly/privately funded Royal Arena, designed by the architecture studio 3XN, that opened in 2017. The Lord Mayor, Frank Jensen, proclaimed that it would be 'massive for the city' as a location to host mega 'community events'. In an interview at Morgen DAC in 2020, the Lord Mayor likened the societal role of the new super arena, where ticket prices range from 300 to more than DKK 5,000, to that of the now largely defunded community centres. (Hermine Trandber)

Recently, the influence of global capital on cultural heritage and housing prices has been heavily debated. Particularly, the US investment fund Blackstone's model of buying up private rental housing, renovating it in an insensitive way and then doubling or even quadrupling the rent has been subject to discussion. However, according to the art historian and architect Kasper Lægring, Blackstone is just one actor among many others who ruins cultural heritage and affordable housing in Copenhagen. This kind of profit-oriented approach has destroyed Holckenhus, among others, with its artist studios that go back to the time of the famous artist Krøyer, and Slagtergårdene, where the satirical artist Robert Storm Petersen grew up.

'(...) in reality, the Holckenhus affair is a logical culmination of decades of systematic undermining of the conservation tools available to the municipality. Mette Frederiksen, Kaare Dybvad and Frank Jensen have preferred to focus on Blackstone as an anomaly, but in Copenhagen preservation-worthy buildings have for decades been free trade for unscrupulous investors, American or not. One saw it coming in the capital, where one 'conservation-worthy' building after another is willingly sacrificed as dominoes – most recently Slagtergårdene on Vesterbro.

Virtually all Social Democrats, including Dybvad, welcomed the development around Slagtergårdene in their time, because the city had an increase in the need for housing, and the roof of Holckenhus housing will be built on the ashes of the artist studios. With liveability, as it were.'

(Kasper Lægring, 'København har selv lokket kapitalfondene til', in *Politiken Byrum*, 9 September 2019)

Astrid Noacks Atelier is an art space on Outer Nørrebro where the artist Astrid Noack lived from 1936 to 1950. Until recently, the studio was part of one of the last preserved courtyard spaces with small businesses and garages – a cultural environment that used to be typical of Copenhagen's 'bridge districts' before the comprehensive urban regeneration of the 1990s. The artist studio has been preserved, but the context has changed following the demolition of the other existing buildings and their replacement with a seven-storey block of flats – in spite of protests from locals and the art community as well as prominent private foundations such as Realdania and Carlsberg. (Laura Stamer and Finn Thybo)

ORG-WARS – THE ARCHITECT AS MEDIATOR

With the exhibition 'org-wars', Crimson, the Dutch office of architectural historians and urbanists, reflects on how architecture moves between different fields, practices and disciplines. They claim that one of the principal roles of the architect, and of other actors working within the field of architecture and urbanism, is increasingly to serve as a mediator. As society becomes more complex and more actors are negotiating the city and the production of space, the ability to navigate between different interests becomes essential.

'The culture of European urbanism in general is based on an ideal sameness of Urbs and Civitas, on the city as a physical artefact being the logical offspring of the city as a discrete governable unit (...) Urbanist discourse in Europe is highly representational of this integrity of government and city-form. It constantly evokes the existence of the city as a coherent mental, physical, political and cultural unit, steered from its civic heart and brain. This explains why the spatial terms used in European urbanism often whisk you away from the streets to a civic never-neverland of dialectical relationships in a phenomenological fog: centre vs. periphery, open vs. enclosed, public vs. private, inside vs. outside etc. (...) We have to admit that the city government is only one of the parties that play in the urban field. In fact now we have many urbes and many civitates. That is, if we accept urbs as simply being the hardware, and civitas the orgware: the collection of organising, regulating and/or financing structures that govern the hardware. These are two distinct levels of urbanity, overlapping in ever new ways, producing new kinds of nodes and unfamiliar landscapes.'

(Crimson – Historians and Urbanists, 'org-wars', text for exhibition by Crimson, The Netherlands-Rotterdam Department of Housing & Planning, https://www.crimsonweb.org/spip.php?article52 accessed 5 June 2020)

The architectural office dominique + serena, formerly known as Studio Fountainhead, was one of the contributors to the manifesto publication *MANIFEST STAFET*, edited by Copenhagen Architecture Festival and the Danish Association of Architects. (dominique + serena: 'Arkitektur er samfundskunst', in *MANIFEST STAFET*. Copenhagen: Forlaget B, 2019)

MANIFESTOS ON THE ROLE OF ARCHITECTURE IN SOCIETY IN THE YEAR 2019

2019 marked the centennial of the opening of the Bauhaus School and the publication of Walter Gropius' seminal Bauhaus manifesto. Copenhagen Architecture Festival and the Danish Association of Architects asked various actors working within the complex field of architecture and urbanism to compose a manifesto that reflects on the role of architecture in society in the year 2019. 49 contributions were compiled in the publication *MANIFEST STAFET.* Claus Bech-Danielsen, professor of architecture at BUILD, Aalborg University, and an expert in the regeneration of modernist social housing estates, contributed with a manifesto to the publication. Over the next 10 years, Bech-Danielsen and his research team at BUILD will follow the transformations of ghetto-labelled social housing estates.

ARCHITECTURE – IDEOLOGY IN SOLID FORM

'Modernism was developed approximately a hundred years ago. It still influences everything that we do in our work with architecture. This is the case whether we build upon the ideals of modernism, or if we create our architecture in direct confrontation with them. Today, for instance, we are reuniting everything that the modernists separated: functions, road users and social classes. The ideology of modernism is up for negotiation too – which also should be the case. However, it must not lead to the misconception that architecture can evade ideological positioning. Architecture cannot be positionless.'

(Claus Bech-Danielsen, 'Arkitektur – ideologi i fast form', in *MANIFEST STAFET* Copenhagen: Copenhagen Architecture Festival, Forlaget B, 2019)

CHALLENGES AND QUESTIONS THE FINGER PLAN – COPENHAGEN'S OLD GLOVE WITH NEW ADJUSTMENTS

Since its launch in 1947, Copenhagen's iconic Finger Plan has been updated several times. In many ways, it has guided Copenhagen's development, although it was never officially adopted as a regional plan. The various adjustments reflect values and ideals of the periods in which they were made. The latest update was made in 2019, causing debate in relation to new settlement patterns with a rise in segregated enclaves, increasing inequality, skyrocketing real estate prices and an overall pressure on Copenhagen.

‘Many homes are being built in Copenhagen, but the high prices are helping to push people out of the city, especially to the surrounding communities, but also farther out. How do we create attractive building plots and housing in several municipalities in the area of the Finger Plan? And do we have to live on more and more square metres or do we need to build less?

In the future, there will be significantly more elderly and single people, but most municipalities do not focus on the older population in their housing development, although it has proved to be a great resource. Most Danes want to live in detached houses, but single people in general and older single people will be more in need of flats.

(...)

Housing development is planned in the municipalities with area restrictions on the part of the state. There is virtually no coordination at the inter-municipal or regional level. Could a greater dialogue be created across municipalities, the state and the region about the regional housing development in the Fingerplan area?’

(Department of Geosciences and Nature Management (IGN) and Danish Urban Planning Laboratory (DB) 2017, Capital 2030-Future challenges for planning in the metropolitan area, p. 4-5)

MANIFESTO. THE ROLE OF ARCHITECTURE IN SOCIETY.

Manifesto by the author Morten Pape first published in Copenhagen Architecture Festival’s publication *MANIFEST STAFET* in 2019.

“The most important societal role of architecture is to create buildings and physical frameworks that speak respectfully to their citizens ”

(Morten Pape in *MANIFEST STAFET*. Copenhagen: Copenhagen Architecture Festival, Publisher B, 2019.)

3.

Urgency

If we look into both the near and the far future, architecture and urbanism are facing a fundamental paradigm shift in their understanding of the new. The modernist 'shock of the new' was a promise to move and shake the world for the better. Today, 'the new' has become a dubious thing as the future does not necessarily hold the same promise of ever more prosperity and growth as the utopia of modernity once promised. Scrambling to overcome the catastrophe and nihilism of WWII, post-war urbanism strove to rebuild Europe based on an understanding of perpetual, limitless progress. The relief of surviving a total collapse only infused the utopian thinking with more energy and idealistic dreaming. Today and in the near future the urgency of the climate crises and the unexpected ramifications of decades of accelerated consumerism supporting mantras of economic growth and globalization are fundamentally challenging modernist urban ideals. With a firm belief in growth and progress, natural resources and basic amenities such as water and clean air were uncritically exploited to realize great master plans to the benefit of mankind – but it left the rest of the world's species behind while exploiting them as resources and means to a human-centered narrative of progress and growth. Thus, we find ourselves in the era of the Anthropocene where one species is deeply affecting the destiny and life conditions of every other form of life on this planet. An impact that we are only gradually realizing but which nonetheless urgently demands a radical reinterpretation of our relation to nature and the meaning of interdependence. A reinterpretation that is also increasingly reflected within urbanism and architecture as the old dichotomy of nature and city slowly loses its meaning, pointing instead towards a future where planning will be a question of managing the responsibilities of multispecies interdependence.

The climate crisis, in particular, forces us to reconsider the goals and means of urbanism in the context of a consumerism-driven wealth state. A hybrid mode of thinking is emerging: the idea of pragmatic utopian thinking. It combines the here-and-now with the ability to think big. It invests itself in concrete problem-solving, while also recognizing the need for urban scenarios that reach far into the future. The threat of rising sea levels to coastal cities all over the world, such as Copenhagen, requires extremely long-term planning, as the urbanist Charles Bessard has pointed out in his research. It threatens the very idea of the city as a safe haven for people, e.g. the future scenarios of newly constructed upper-middle class urban neighbourhoods like Nordhavn, Islands Brygge and Sluseholmen with their location close to the harbour. The investments in infrastructure and adaptation for the effects of extreme precipitation are enormous, and changing transport and settlement patterns will be difficult.

Copenhagen's success as a bike- and tourist-friendly city with clean harbour water all of a sudden seems irrelevant in the light of these mounting challenges. The city as primarily a functional diagram of well-functioning infrastructure and urban spaces that planning professionals could optimize – let alone control – is less relevant in the 21st century as the perspective has changed. Now ideology, justice and moralism (again) take centre stage in the planning discussion. Of course, rational planning is needed in order to protect cities from the rising sea levels, but the cost will be high and detrimental to the celebrated lifestyle ideals of the welfare city as we know it. Thus, future planning schemes will have to strike a balance between social justice in a time of rising inequality, the broader question of care in the wake of the global COVID-19 pandemic and simultaneously adapting to the expected extreme conditions of climate changes. Transformation of the existing building mass, circularity, resource minimalism, communityand urban biodiversity will dramatically expand the field and aim of the planning profession and change the face of the wealth city with its consumerism, urban branding and profit.

Influential contemporary architect Rem Koolhaas (b. 1944), the Dutch founder of the architectural office OMA and its congenial counterpart, the research office AMO, embraces political, cultural and economic events and trends in his buildings and writings. On September 24 2014, Koolhaas spoke at a High Level Group meeting on Smart Cities in Brussels. He critically addresses the shift in the architect's involvement in city-making and the quiet, yet fundamental change in the underlying narratives of city development during the past decades.

'Architecture used to be about the creation of community, and making the best effort at symbolizing that community. Since the triumph of the market economy in the late 1970s, architecture no longer expresses public values but instead the values of the private sector. It is in fact a regime – the ¥€$ regime – and it has invaded every domain, whether we want it or not. This regime has had a very big impact on cities and the way we understand cities. With safety and security as selling points, the city has become vastly less adventurous and more predictable. To compound the situation, when the market economy took hold at the end of the 1970s, architects stopped writing manifestos. We stopped thinking about the city at the exact moment of the explosion in urban substance in the developing world. The city triumphed at the very moment that thinking about the city stopped. The "smart" city has stepped into that vacuum.

(...)

COMFORT, SECURITY, SUSTAINABILITY

Because the smart city movement has been apolitical in its declarations, we also have to ask about the politics behind the improvements on offer. A new trinity is at work: traditional European values of liberty, equality, and fraternity have been replaced in the 21st century by comfort, security, and sustainability. They are now the dominant values of our culture, a revolution that has barely been registered.'

(Rem Koolhaas, edited transcript of talk at High Level Group meeting on Smart Cities, Brussels, 24 September 2014 – Originally published by the European Commission as part of their 'Digital Minds for a New Europe' series, https://ec.europa.eu/archives/commission_2010-2014/kroes/en/content/my-thoughts-smart-city-rem-koolhaas.html accessed 5 March 2020)

Security measures against urban terrorism and the elimination of 'man-made' risk constitute new dimensions of welfare urbanism, implying a series of new perspectives on community, belonging, trust, democracy, norms of conduct in public space and the open society. This development was fuelled by the seminal event of 9/11 in New York in 2001 and subsequently spread as a global 'War on Terror'. Here, professor of urbanism at KADK, Deane Simpson, considers how securitization influences Copenhagen's urban design and the regulation of behaviour in public space.

> 'As a framework for our daily lives the public spaces of the city are fragile systems, sensitive to the impacts and dynamics of the insidious security controls. They increasingly appear as permanent measures such as bollards, barriers, planters, surveillance systems, gates, fences, or guard posts – measures representing a particular way of thinking that positions itself somewhere between architecture, risk management and criminology. Abroad this new security-thinking has had consequences for the ambience and spatial qualities of public space; the way in which the space is used; its ability to support social relations; the activities that are permitted or tolerated in the space; and also the political and symbolic associations of the space to ideals such as openness, trust, democracy, etc. There is therefore reason to consider what is at stake when we engage with the all but impossible project of eliminating the risk of terrorist acts by fortifying our public space – complex places, where a determined perpetrator has almost infinite opportunities for inflicting harm.'

(Deane Simpson, 'Sikkerhed og arkitektur 3: Frihed eller komfort', blog post on *Arkitekten*'s website 28 January 2020, https://arkitektforeningen.dk/arkitekten/sikkerhed-og-arkitektur-3-frihed-eller-komfort/ accessed 11 June 2020)

GHB Landscape Architects designed the giant stone necklace in 2019 as a protection of the square in front of the Danish Parliament, a feature that safeguards the parliament and manifestations on the square from motorized terrorist attacks while securing public accessibility to the space. Hence, the square with the statue of Frederik VII, the king who granted the Danes democracy in 1849, is frequently used for demonstrations. (Courtesy of GHB Landscape Architects)

While researching for an architecture competition Syrian architect Wesam Asali, experienced how his otherwise normal behaviour in public space was criminalized under the imperative of security due to his ethnic background.

> 'I was taking photos of a building that was a site of an architectural competition, it appeared that the building was near a police station. Two police patrols stopped. A friendly conversation unexpectedly accelerated when my identity was declared: I am Syrian. I remember very well when the police officer asked, just before he handcuffed me: "Don't you think it is dangerous that a Syrian is taking photos near a police station during these days?"
>
> (...)
>
> This "precautious arrest" (sic), as one detective phrased it while interrogating me and scrolling through my mobile content, did have a huge impact on changing how I see Copenhagen after almost five years of living and working in the city. It was no longer a place where I could enjoy the same accessibility to its facilities, public spaces and urban life like a Copenhagener, I realised.'

(Wesam Asali, *Temporal Pandemic, Perpetual Identity: A Personal Account of the Inaccessible City*, 2020 https://cafx.dk/corona-essays/temporal-pandemic/)

In the essay 'A City of Comings and Goings', the Dutch office Crimson challenges the predominant view on migration in the wake of the so-called refugee crisis in 2015 that allegedly swept the Western cities and societies as an unwelcome surprise. However, learning from history, Crimson argues that migration and mobility of different groups of migrants, ranging from expats to students, urban nomads, empty-nesters, refugees and seasonal workers, have always affected urban development by their continuous comings and goings.

> '(But) we can be sure that migrants in all their diverse guises will become ever more present and that "the system" will be forced to change. The distinction between the migrant and non-migrant will be blurred and the common ground between the refugee, the asylum seeker, the immigrant, the migrant worker, the research fellow, the student, the guest professor, the intern, the au pair and the pied-à-terre owner will become increasingly clear. And that common ground is that they lead a flexible and uncertain existence in which their adaptability and mobility is crucial to achieving the happiness they seek.
>
> If the future unfolds as outlined above, our cities will increasingly be characterised by a coming and going of people, population growth and contraction, the emergence and disappearance of amenities and enterprises, and a constantly changing racial profile.'
>
> (Wouter Vanstiphout and Michelle Provoost, 'A City of Comings and Goings', CRIMSON Historians and urbanists, 2015, https://www.crimsonweb.org/spip.php?article215 accessed 11 June 2020)

In the aftermath of the 'refugee crisis' when non-European refugees were walking the highways of EU countries, including Denmark, accommodation for the new refugees became a major issue. ONV Architects designed a new housing typology with joint facilities, combining two groups of newcomers to the city who both have a hard time finding affordable housing – students and refugees. In ONV's project, students become buddies for their refugee housemates, stimulating integration and dialogue in the everyday living environment. In short, the goal is to see the refugees as a resource that should be integrated in society rather than being isolated in camps. In 2019, the project 'The Friendly Dwelling Plus' was realized on Frederiksberg in collaboration with the social housing associations Frederiksbergs Forenede Boligselskaber and KAB. (Courtesy of ONV Architects)

Originally, Sjælsmark functioned as military barracks, designed by the architect K. Jensen-Gaard in the beginning of the 1950s, during the Cold War when Denmark joined NATO in 1949 and expanded the military facilities. After the soldiers left the well-preserved brick buildings in 2005, Sjælsmark became an accommodation centre for refugees. Since February 2015, Sjælsmark has functioned as an exit centre for rejected refugees. Isolated from the outside world by fences in an otherwise idyllic and wealthy part of North Zealand, they are contained before being forced to return to their country of origin. In general, there is a 'duty to stay' in the exit centre, but the rejected asylum seekers can get permission to leave the centre on rare occasions. Meals are served in a cafeteria, and children can get snacks. Sjælsmark is managed by the Probation Service (Kriminalforsorgen). (Signe Sophie Bøggild)

In the book *Living Complex: From Zombie City to the New Communal* (2015), the German author and architect Niklas Maak reflects on how ideals and needs of housing are affected by the dramatic demographic changes as society becomes more heterogeneous, lifestyles are diversifying and the good life must be written in the plural. As new 'household configurations' evolve, architects, developers, decision-makers etc. must rethink the design of housing.

'The standardization of lifestyles has its equivalent in the standardization of public spaces that surrounds residential buildings (...) State housing associations, real estate developers, and builders ask too seldom for whom they are really building. They ignore the fact that Western societies are aging rapidly, resulting in a population that no longer has the same spatial and financial resources as previous generations and must live at a reduced scale simply because of economic constraints. And they ignore another important demographic trend: society is heading toward a point where the classic family no longer represents the majority. In other words, they are building for a lifestyle that no longer exists as such.

(...) According to an analysis by the German Federal Institute of Demography, Germany is among the countries with the highest percentage of single-person households, about 40 percent, of all countries in Europe – only Norway and Denmark ranked higher. In the major cities the number was even over 50 percent in 2011; in Berlin and Munich, families are by now almost a marginal group – their share of all households no more than between 14 and 20 percent.

How do politicians, planners, architects and builders respond to this fundamental change?'

(Niklas Maak: *Living Complex: From Zombie City to the New Communal*. Munich: Hirmer, 2015, pp. 14-15)

In 2019, the Danish Arts Foundation and the philanthropic association Realdania launched a new 'Housing Laboratory'. The initiative seeks to restart Danish housing design as a response to the challenges to the long tradition of quality, innovative design and affordability that have faced the built environment over the past three or four decades. The Housing Laboratory has invited actors in the building industry to develop new concepts and typologies of housing. Five to seven prototypes will be selected for realization to provide experimental demonstrations of new solutions for construction and housing design. The project is planned for completion in 2025, but critics warn that the project's innovative potential cannot be fulfilled due to regulations limiting experimentation.

> 'In Denmark, 37 different family forms are now registered. It in itself calls for new forms of living and ways to create space for the community. Between 30 and 40% of the total greenhouse gas emissions in Denmark are stemming from construction. It also calls for radically new ways of building and living that respond to specific challenges and take into account both geography, identity, demographics and local communities.'

(Realdania, Press release: New housing laboratory to restart Danish housing construction, 18 Dec 2019)

Carsten Hoff is an architect who has experimented with alternative housing models and coexistence throughout his career (including with Susanne Ussing in Thylejren). Challenging building and planning regulations, he argues in favour of allowing people freedom to experiment. In a discussion article in the newspaper *Politiken* from 2019, Hoff advocates customizing housing design and construction to offer possibilities beyond the more large-scale developers' generic dwelling designs, which are often dictated by estate agents and the average norms of the (white) middle-class nuclear family.

'In the City of Copenhagen's housing policy manifesto 2017–2025, "Architecture for people", it says that one intends to develop the diverse city by promoting the planning of functionally mixed urban neighbourhoods, including a varied retail life, and allowing areas in new local plans to be offered as small plots to create variety and room for smaller initiatives and building communities (...) The will to diversity is clearly present, but why are the intentions not put into practice? Is it the metro financing agreement? An agreement in which, with the CPH City & Port Development, they sell at market price and use the profit to finance the metro and other infrastructure. An agreement in which the plots offered are designed for developers who are not interested in the small scale but in large-scale building. Yet, it may not be true that the choice in today's urban development is between metro and diverse residential areas. Since the city cannot afford to relinquish the quality that construction on the small scale can bring, the urban politicians have to think again. It is discouraging to invest in quantity and finances in the short term.'

(Carsten Hoff, 'Nybyggeriet i København er dødssygt og monotont – lad os dog få lidt spræl og variation', *Politiken*, 26 March 2019)

Designed by Praksis Architects and completed in 2018, ‘Byfællesskabet’ is a private building cooperative forming an L shape around a small public garden. It is part of the ongoing reclaiming of Odense’s central Thomas B. Thriges Gade, a modernist mega-infrastructure project which used to cut the city in two halves. The rooftop covering the two connected volumes of the building are partly covered by greenery as part of the local rainwater management plan but mostly forms the common garden for the building cooperative outside the penthouse common room. The joint project was built without kitchens, so that each family can organize their own and decide how much money they want to spend or contribute with their own labour for finishes. (Silje Erøy Sollien)

Silje Erøy Sollien, an industrial post.doc. at Vandkunsten Architects and Aalborg University, interviews the high-school teacher Janus Lylloff, who has realized his dream of building an alternative housing community in the middle of Odense, inspired by the German model of the independent *Baugruppen*, without involving a professional developer. Byfællesskabet offers an example of how private initiatives can create new types of housing and community. The housing collective brings together residents between the ages of 7 and 70, and demonstrates the possibility of alternative financing and collaborative dynamics between top-down (Odense Municipality) and bottom-up planning for new housing.

'After a process of five years and meetings every two weeks, nine families could move into "Byfællesskabet", a building where they had designed each flat individually and managed to realize some communal design choices you would never find in the normal housing market. (...) "The normal market doesn't build for people like me. I am a common family father and don't have particular purchasing power," he adds. Janus teaches math and physics in upper secondary school and has no experience as property developer. However, when he saw the public offering of plots right next to what is now Hotel Odeon for a housing project, he called the architect Mette Tony from Praksis Architects and placed a tender to develop the plot as a private building cooperative.

Janus invited people to information meetings in the evenings in a community centre. There was an over-representation of a certain type of future residents at the meetings, people of 60 years+ who watched the local news and read local newspapers. "The families with toddlers do not have time to read the local media and are very difficult to reach," Janus explains. He even went to playgrounds to chat to families with small children about his project, but by the time the contract was signed with an entrepreneur, there was still one flat missing for a family with small children.

The first phase of the selection process for the house community was concluded with help from two consultants at Kuben Management, who held a full day workshop for the potential members of the building cooperative to assess common values and strategies. The workshop allowed Janus to step back and let an anthropologist lead the group and help find the six families that could fit together with the same vision and expectations for a housing community. After starting the drawing process, it became clear that the building could fit nine families. The flats range from $77m^2$ to $116m^2$, with $12.5m^2$ common area per flat, including a large common dining room and lounge. There are guest rooms and a large common rooftop terrace in two levels covering the whole building.

"We have made some particular choices because WE are the residents", Janus says. The common room can be completely opened up to the front terrace with large folding doors, a choice no cost-minimizing developer would have made. The most expensive square metres in terms of potential sales revenue are given to the common room, with great views over the entire city to both sides. The members of "Byfællesskabet" eat together here once a week. The cooking groups are formed across flats, so that you don't cook together with your wife or partner.

(...)

"If one were to do this in the future, one should have a professional to do the job I have done! If you use a project leader who knows the building industry and some law, someone who could say, 'this is the way you do it in the building industry', one could build this type of project in two years, not five," Janus concludes with hindsight.'

(Excerpts from an interview with Janus Lylloff, initiator and resident in the housing collective Byfællesskabet in Odense, by Silje Erøy Sollien)

BOTTOM-UP

Citizen participation is a complicated thing. Mandate, process and motivation often need more transparency than what is usually the case – particularly in times of crisis. Here, a comment by Chiara Dorbolò, architect and researcher at Failed Architecture, NL, warning of the risk of private initiatives becoming an alibi for local authorities to make cheaper and less sustainable short-term solutions.

'Concepts like social sustainability, community participation and city-making are usually very popular during times of economic crisis when local governments tend to be supportive of practices that offer low-cost, bottom-up and often temporary solutions to urban problems. Yet there is a tendency to use these terms to support projects and interventions led by financial motives rather than social ones ...

(...) As already mentioned, the problem starts with the word itself, participation, and its inability to translate into reasonable benchmarks. With a focus on the process and not the result, and its complete lack of information on *if* and *how* participants will be able to exert an impact, the word participation seems to lend itself well to empty advertising. Indeed, words are important, and we should prefer less ambiguous, more result-oriented ones like "co-creation" or "co-design". At any rate, not only institutions, developers and architects should make an effort to define the terms that they use upfront, but communities and those who make efforts to defend them should also be wary of how their work might be used within profit-driven developments.'

(Chiara Dorbolò, 'We Participate, They Profit', 6 March 2020 on Failed Architecture's website: https://failedarchitecture.com/we-participate-they-profit/ accessed 24 March 2020)

THE CITY IN THE ERA OF CLIMATE CHANGE

In his debut novel *Solar*, Theis Ørntoft writes about life in the age of the Anthropocene and the climate crisis. Hiking on the pilgrimage route Hærvejen in Jutland, the protagonist Theis describes the cosmic experience of a world where the usual binaries of nature and culture, past and present collapse.

'Everything is woven together and connected. Everything has causes, everything has effects in a confusing, multidimensional tissue.

Man has no language for that which is happening.

My life is part of this confusion.

The private is not political.

The private is planetary.'

(Theis Ørntoft: *Solar*. Copenhagen: Gyldendal. 2018, quoted from Tue Andersen Nexø, 'Theis Ørntoft har skrevet et kosmisk hærværk af en roman', in *Information*, 23 March 2018)

In 2014, the Dutch landscape architect Dirk Sijmons was curator of the Rotterdam Biennale, entitled *Urban By Nature*. The biennale reflected on how nature and culture, urban and rural are no longer opposites in the age of the Anthropocene.

'Since the declaration of the Anthropocene, we no longer have to maintain the fiction of a division between what is natural and what is artificial. We can face the fact that they are closely intertwined. We can also acknowledge that many of the processes around us are in fact hybrids: combinations in which both "natural" and "human" forces are at work. What we have hitherto dubbed "natural" is *also* artificial, and what we used to call "artificial" is *also* natural. This applies to land use, river and ocean currents, flora and fauna, to the climate, and it also applies to one of the biggest and most visible hybrid forms on earth: the urban landscape. The simplistic arrangement of the past, in which we had placed city and nature in opposition to each other so that they excluded each other, is no longer valid. Perhaps we humans are "by nature" inclined to live together in expanding settlements – perhaps we are *urban by nature*. That insight liberates us from a lot of moralistic brooding about "good" and "bad" in the relationship between nature and city.

In the Anthropocene we realize that city and nature overlap spatially and impact each other functionally. For spatial designers this is a unique challenging situation. What opportunities do these new hybrid forms present for organizing the urban landscape in an appealing and livable way? What new terminology can we use to discuss the city in the Anthropocene? What are the prospects for action for planners, nature conservationists, landscape architects, and urban designers?'

(Dirk Sijmons, 'Waking up in the Antropocene', 2014, https://iabr.nl/en/curator/c2014antropoceen accessed 6 March 2020)

Manifesto by partner in the architectural studio Tredje Natur (Third Nature) Flemming Rafn Thomsen. Transgressing the habitual dichotomies of nature/culture, city/countryside, Tredje Natur is an innovative practice specializing in projects such as Enghaveparken, which is designed to manage extreme precipitation. The manifesto was part of Copenhagen Architecture Festival and the Danish Association of Architects' publication *MANIFEST STAFET.*

'With Walter Gropius' Bauhaus manifesto in 1919, the complete building artwork was elevated as the ultimate goal of all art forms. By reuniting craft with architecture, art was going to play a fundamental role in the development of society.

(...)

It is well known that it was not art, but industry and capital that were the prime mover of urban development. And just like the hand, losing its relation to the machine, the urbanization process totally lost the connection to the organic foundation. The cities were insensitively founded on top of life-critical ecosystems with a resource-wise and climatically very high price. Today, it is clear that the ongoing success of urbanization is dependent on a basis without perspective for humanity, where construction, buildings and infrastructure together constitute the greatest impact on the planet.

The last time there was so much CO_2 in the atmosphere was several million years ago and the normal water level was 15-25 metres higher than it is today. And there is no immediate prospect of any rapid deflection of the accelerating discharge. The Bitcoin system alone uses more power than what all of the planet's solar cells generate, the California forest fires emit more CO_2 annually than the entire electricity consumption of the US, and the construction activities in China alone have used more cement in the last three years than the US throughout the 20th century. In addition, cities are expected to continue to grow steadily at an unprecedented rate towards the 22nd century.

(...)

Thus, there is a need for a climate ethical design pragmatics among architects, at once aiming to address behaviour, discharge and adaptation in one and the same movement. Where each architectural project ultimately presents a transparent and engaging narrative, connecting us to the ecological and behavioural ethical contexts. And through this lifts all of us into an exposed field between creation and destruction.'

(Flemming Rafn Thomsen, Tredje Natur, 'Et involverende narrativ', in *MANIFEST STAFET*. Copenhagen: Copenhagen Architecture Festival, Forlaget B, 2019)

The historic park Enghaveparken is now Copenhagen's largest climate project. With a 22,600-m3 water reservoir, the park responds to future water challenges. The challenges are positively transformed into a wide range of new living, sensory and movement options to be used both in everyday life and in case of cloudbursts. (Courtesy of Tredje Natur)

The future of the city is highly dependent on planning, and the planning discipline has a hard time grasping the risk scenarios unfolding in the wake of climate change. In his recent PhD dissertation, the architect Charles Bessard studied the consequences of rising sea levels. In view of the crises and risks currently challenging the development of the city and society, and in particular the climate changes that are transforming the entire globe, Charles Bessard advocates a more long-term planning than what is usually the case today but was favoured by modernists like Le Corbusier and Constantinos Doxiadis.

Kristoffer Weiss: It requires an extremely long planning perspective to tackle the issues you are studying?

Charles Bessard: What's interesting is that it projects an extremely long lifespan at a time where urban development is really struggling with long lifespans. We are in a very strange paradox, where on the one hand we are facing a totally unprecedented situation, which for a low-lying city like Copenhagen could potentially have an extreme impact. If we think that in 2200, many of the scenarios are projecting a sea level rise of four metres. Current city extensions, such as Nordhavn, will be flooded. So, on the one hand we have our short-term economic interests. And in terms of planning, 30 or 40 years is long-term – short-term is maybe five years. But in terms of geology, these are extremely short terms. We're developing areas that are very attractive with a high quality of life, or livability, because they are by the seaside. But they are also areas that are potential future flood zones. So we have this extreme tension between the immediate economic interests, and that will have a strong green profile but raises questions of robustness and durability in the long term. It shows how this economic dimension of sustainability and green growth can become very questionable.

Kristoffer Weiss: And it will undermine or challenge ideas of liveability, will fundamentally influence how we organize the city, how we move around in the city?

Charles Bessard: Yes. Climate change means risk. An interesting aspect of risk is: who takes the risk? Who benefits? And who pays the price? Flood risk is actually quite interesting, because we tend to understand it as a natural risk. Yet, there is no risk when nothing is lost. When you have flooding in a field where there is nothing, then there is no risk. So basically you can say, of course there is a risk with climate change, but it comes mostly from what we do in the flood plains. If we build a house, we create risk. When we put people in coastal areas, which are very attractive but potentially exposed to floods, we create risk. And this risk, when it comes to sea level rise, is for later. So the people who actually profit by building, buying, selling these apartments are not the ones that will be exposed to the risk. So it's a question of ethics.

(Charles Bessard, 'Liveability in the Age of the Risk City', interview with Kristoffer Weiss in *Critical City*. The Danish Architectural Press, 2019, pp. 280-281)

Pioneering sustainability solutions and commitment to the 17 SDGs were the decisive factors securing Lendager Group's bid to design the UN17 Village: 400 new homes in Copenhagen, planned to be realized in 2023 and concluding 25 years of development of the new city district, Ørestad South. So far, the focus in sustainable buildings has mainly been on their operational carbon emissions. 'We are looking at the whole life cycle of the building – including materials use, health and quality of life,' explains Anders Lendager, CEO and founder of Lendager Group. (Courtesy of Lendager Group)

As the necessary steps to mitigate the effects of climate change are not being taken on national governmental levels, 96 cities around the world have joined the C40 network in an attempt to implement green policies and exchange best practices. Copenhagen's brand of a liveable and climate-conscious city was intensely promoted and widely applauded during the Copenhagen Summit in 2019, although several mayors of the Global South pointed out that the infrastructural deficits, lack of resources, precarious living conditions and more severe effects from climate change faced by their cities made such cases unrealistic references.

> 'The climate crisis is a reality. Every day city governments experience problems caused by the climate crisis. Everywhere there are heavy rain, strong hurricanes or extreme heat waves. We have all felt that the climate is changing. Our citizens know it too. Young people by the million are taking to the streets, demanding change.
>
> (...)
>
> Cities are central to achieving the Paris agreement. Accounting for almost 80% of the energy consumption and 75% of the global greenhouse gas emissions. When cities act, it makes a difference. Around the world, C40 cities are taking bold climate actions, leading the way towards a healthier and more sustainable future, while at the same time improving the well-being of their citizens. In Copenhagen, as Connie (Hedegaard, ed.) told you, we want to become the first carbon neutral capital city by 2025. It *is* very ambitious, but we have already come a long way.'
>
> (Opening remarks by Lord Mayor of Copenhagen, Frank Jensen, at the C40 World Mayors Summit in Copenhagen, October 2019)

With their usual approach of combining the practical/pragmatic and the hedonistic, BIG has designed a hybrid of an incinerator, hiking trails and a ski slope in Copenhagen – something hitherto missing in the pancake-flat country of Denmark. The futuristic project is part of the city's ambition of becoming a carbon-neutral capital in 2025, rhyming with its agenda of liveability. Meanwhile, developments sometimes outdo the relative slowness of architecture. Recently, the municipality has announced a future strategy of recycling waste rather than burning it. (Stills from Kaspar Astrup Schröder's film 'Making a Mountain', which will be premiering in 2020)

COPENHILL – HEDONISTIC SUSTAINABILITY

Famous for its roof ski slope, the Copenhagen waste plant merges fantasies of the liveable city with the complex task of waste management. Critical voices note that times are changing with focus shifting from traditional waste systems to radical recycling. Either way, CopenHill turns a black dot on the map into a leisire landscape, becoming the very symbol of a city where 'you can have both'.

> 'Fun factory? We propose a new breed of waste-to-energy plant, one that is economically, environmentally, and socially profitable. Instead of considering Amager Ressource Center as an isolated architectural object, we consider the assignment to design a facade as an opportunity for the local context.
>
> Alpine skiing in Copenhagen: we propose to turn the roof of the new Amager Ressource Center into an artificial ski slope for the citizens of Copenhagen, where it will be possible to ski all year round! The ski slope will be ecological, upending the convention of energy intensive indoor or alpine ski resort.'

(BIG's description of CopenHill/Amager Bakke,
BIG's website: https://big.dk/#projects-arc accessed 30 March 2020)

Alexander Hadley, a writer and architect based in Barcelona, wonders just how generous and beneficial for the environment projects labelled as sustainable by architects like BIG really are, despite their good intentions.

> 'The CopenHill waste-burning ski slope, featured in a recent car commercial for Ford, encapsulates in many ways the dynamic of well funded sustainable-minded architecture. While a plant that incinerates waste to produce electricity is certainly a better option to the alternative methods of disposal, it is only a temporary solution that allows one to sidestep the larger and more difficult issue of industrial waste generation that is rapidly degrading the biosphere. Attaching an expensive sports facility on top adds a secondary layer of distance from the serious scale of response required to address the climate crisis. The sustainable elements of these projects are an improvement, but the value is overwritten by their unwillingness to confront the deeper ecological issues of the architecture industry. The truth is that behind the facade of high-minded architectural theories of utopia or pragmatism or even sustainability, a more powerful cultural force is at work, the same force that prompted the emphasis on sustainability in the first place.'

(Alexander Hadley, 'Bjarke Ingels and the Art of Greenwashing', article of Failed Architecture's website 28 January 2020: https://failedarchitecture.com/bjarke-ingels-and-the-art-of-greenwashing/ accessed 30 March 2020)

Human beings are not the only ones finding it hard to find adequate accommodation in Copenhagen. This swan by the Sortedam Lake and other species are also struggling, and biodiversity is an aspect of the ongoing fight to make the city more sustainable for all. (Signe Sophie Bøggild)

The Covid-19 pandemic and the resulting health crisis changed our behaviour in and regulation of public space in a split second after the lockdown of society in March 2020. In this comment, Sibylle Buhl Karottki from GHB Landscape Architects reflects on the impact of corona on the design of the city of the future.

'Could it be that politicians have now opened their eyes to the importance of prioritizing green spaces in urban development? That the behaviour currently unfolding in urban spaces could lead to a reconsideration of the design of the future city?

Good urban spaces are always in demand – both during and after the corona crisis. Intelligent urban development, where city and nature aren't in opposition, enhances the well-being of the residents and is an important aspect of the climate challenges that we are still in the midst of. Increased volumes of rain can actually be managed quite poetically so that they creates value rather than problems and contribute with lushness and biodiversity.

Therefore, let us not forget the potential of urban space when we plan for the city of tomorrow. Of course, we need roofs over our heads, but residents also use the city, they move around and sojourn. That is why they live here.'

(Sibylle Buhl Karottki, 'Coronaen afslører de gode og de dårlige byrum', 13 May 2020, *Politiken Byrum*: https://politikenbyrum.dk/Debat/art7779522/Coronaen-afsl%C3%B8rer-de-gode-og-de-d%C3%A5rlige-byrum accessed 11 June 2020)

The Covid-19 virus changed our behaviour in public space and further exposed the segregation and inequalities within society, while a new financial crisis is already kicking in. The graffiti in front of Assistens Cemetery on Nørrebro reads 'Let the rich people pay for Covid-19'. (Signe Sophie Bøggild)

THE RETURN OF PANDEMICS: CORONAVIRUS, (UN)CARE AND INEQUALITY

In a recent essay, the American philosopher Judith Butler reflects on the paradoxes of belonging and borders during the Covid-19 crisis. A comment that is even more thought-provoking after the police murder of George Floyd in the U.S. and the global responses to (racial) injustice.

> 'What are the consequences of this pandemic for thinking about equality, global interdependence and our obligations toward one another? The virus does not discriminate. We could say that it treats us equally, puts us equally at risk of falling ill, losing someone close, living in a world of imminent threat. By the way it moves and strikes, the virus demonstrates that the human community is equally precarious. At the same time, however, the failure of some states or regions to prepare in advance (the US is now perhaps the most notorious member of that club), the bolstering of national policies and the closing of borders (often accompanied by panicked xenophobia), and the arrival of entrepreneurs eager to capitalize on global suffering, all testify to the rapidity with which radical inequality, which includes nationalism, white supremacy, violence against women, queer, and trans people, and capitalist exploitation find ways to reproduce and strengthen their powers within the pandemic zones This should come as no surprise.'

(Judith Butler, 'Capitalism has its Limits', blog post on Verso website 19 March 2020: https://www.versobooks.com/blogs/4603-capitalism-has-its-limits accessed 24 March 2020)

The French sociologist Bruno Latour thinks beyond the usual questions and dilemmas of the corona crisis of spring 2020, linking it to issues of the larger climate crisis, globalization, modes of production and capitalism, by asking what we might want to get rid of and what we want to keep after the health crisis.

> 'Hence the primary importance for using this time of imposed isolation in order to describe, initially one by one, then as a group, what we are attached to; what we are ready to give up; the chains we are ready to reconstruct and those that, in our behaviour, we have decided to interrupt. As for the globalisers, they seem to have a very clear idea of what they want to see coming back post-crisis: the same but worse, fossil fuel industries and giant cruise ships as a bonus. It is up to us to confront them with a counter-inventory. If in a month or two, millions of humans are capable of learning how to "social distance" at the blow of a whistle, to space themselves for greater solidarity, to stay home so as not to overload the hospitals, then it is easy to imagine the power of transformation that these new protective measures have against bringing back business as usual, or worse, against another battering from those who want to escape from terrestrial attraction forever.'

(Bruno Latour, 'What protective measures can you think of so we don't go back to the pre-crisis production model?': http://www.bruno-latour.fr/sites/default/files/downloads/P-202-AOC-ENGLISH_1.pdf accessed 6 April 2020)

Still photo from *Interdependence: A portrait of Stockholm during COVID-19*, a film portrait of Stockholm during Covid-19 by Studio Reko that examines the effects of the pandemic and Sweden's unilateral approach to corona in relation to the legacy of the Swedish welfare city and state. (Stills from *Interdependence* (2020) by James Taylor-Foster, Franks Wiklund and Ludwig Mattsson. A film by Studio Reko)

MANIFESTO FOR THE HEROES OF THE 21ST CENTURY

Below is a manifesto by Dan Stubbergaard, partner of the architectural office COBE, in which he reflects on the role of the architect in the 21st century. COBE was architectural lead in the development of Copenhagen's new neighbourhood Nordhavn and has designed welfare institutions such as the library in Nordvest and the new community-cum-library in Tingbjerg, among numerous other public projects. As such, COBE is an influential contributor to the development of the welfare city and its architectural traditions and heritage.

'The architect has been announced as the 21st Century villain. And rightly so, perhaps. By way of our visions and convincing abilities winding city centres have been eradicated in favour of efficient high-rises in glass and concrete, situated stringently shoulder by shoulder on an even surface.

(...)

Perhaps it's time to replace the role of the villain with a more heroic role. Time that we decide to save the architecture of the 21st Century from speculation, tedious standards, low-ceilinged flats with no soul, and lifeless urban spaces (...) The challenges facing the world are queing up: climate changes and green transition, urbanization and social segregation, conversion from market economy to a circular economy – just to mention a few. There is an all-pervasive need to change the way we organize our physical world. As Gropius manifested it a 100 years ago: we can build our way to a better world?

(...)

We should all consider what materials we use when we build. But the more sustainable option is to dare ask oneself the question: why build new at all? And when the solution is to build new, does it then create real improvement; does the space become significantly better, or is it yet another unavailing construction that neither moves us, unites us or renews us as human beings but merely, when all comes to all, is a waste of the planet's resources? That question should and must we all ask ourselves.

(...)

We must fight the architecture of carelessness, prove that the meaningful, beautiful, robust architecture can create extraordinary everyday lives for us human beings. Everyday life and the physical world are like two intimately connected vessels. If created with empathy, it has such a remarkable value to us humans that we can help one another raise our gaze above the templates of the excel sheets, the short-term bottom line, the four-year election period, which today define the design of our physical world to a much too great extent.

The architect shall again be the hero of everyday life.'

(Dan Stubbergaard, COBE, *MANIFEST STAFET*, Copenhagen: Copenhagen Architecture Festival, Forlaget B, 2019)

EXCAVATING UTOPIA

Professor in Urban Studies at Roskilde University (RUC) David Pinder reflects on the legacy of utopian movements such as the avant-garde group Situationist International. Despite certain failures, the social visions of the modernists and the avant-garde might serve as an inspiration for how to address the challenges and crises of today.

'Exploring different utopian positions and their potentialities encourages a reconsideration of the value of utopianism in the present. Saying this is not, of course, to deny the many dangers of utopian approaches, including the risk of sounding a nostalgic note for singular pictures of the future or for supposedly stable and adequate representations of a "good society", those "dreams of unity"... As recent debates in social and cultural thought have shown, it is imperative to recognise the partiality of theoretical and political positions as well as the multiplicities and radical uncertainties of the future. Yet one of the compelling features revealed by returning to the utopian visions of the situationists and especially Constant is the way in which they worked with the tensions and difficulties of opening up other spaces rather than assuming they could be fully worked out in an ideal form.'

(David Pinder, *Visions of the city*. Edinburgh University Press, 2005, p. 257)

Shortly before corona conquered cities all over the world, Rem Koolhaas' exhibition 'Countryside: The Future' opened at Guggenheim in New York. With its compilation of case studies, collaborators and perspectives, the exhibition is OMA's manifesto on 'the radical changes in the rural, remote and wild territories collectively identified here as "countryside," or the 98% of the Earth's surface not occupied by cities.' A topic and space that has played second fiddle to research on booming cities, and which has roughly been looked upon as a static terra incognita.

'A central thesis of "Countryside: The Future" is that our current form of urban life has necessitated the organization, abstraction, and automation of the countryside at an unprecedented scale. Data storage, fulfillment centers, genetic engineering, artificial intelligence, robotic automation, economic innovation, worker migration, and the private purchase of land for ecological preservation are in many cases more actively explored and experimented with in the countryside than the city.

(...)

Rem Koolhaas: "In the past decades, I have noticed that while much of our energies and intelligence have been focused on the urban areas of the world—under the influence of global warming, the market economy, American tech companies, African and European initiatives, Chinese politics, and other forces—the countryside has changed almost beyond recognition.

(...)

As soon as we leave the urban condition behind us, we confront newness and the profoundly unfamiliar.

Currently, scientists are developing models in, broadly, two versions. The first, "Half Earth," is based on E. O. Wilson's 2016 manifesto. It implies a drastic separation between an almost pristine nature on the one hand and human habitation and cultivation on the other. The second, "Shared Planet," proposes a more intensive mixing of all our territories. Both approaches imply radical changes in food production, ideology, and agricultural techniques. They will also require the intense collaboration of all spheres, and all political factions that are barely on speaking terms today—and the collective mobilization of tools and technologies that have been spoilt by their unquestioned dominance.'

(https://oma.eu/projects/countryside-the-future accessed 9 June 2020)

POSTHUMAN UTOPIA ON LOLLAND

The prose of the Danish author Kaspar Colling Nielsen addresses topics such as segregation and social stigmatization, urbanization and demographic changes of the periphery, climate change and the Anthropocene, local effects of global capitalism and technology, changes of the welfare society etc. in surrealist and futuristic ways. In satirical scenarios, reminiscent of societal fables like Voltaire's Candide, he examines issues of contemporary society in sci-fi settings that turn the order of things upside down. Below is an excerpt of the novel *The European Spring* (2017), where Colling Nielsen stages a conversation between two talking animals from a near future discussing a fictive makeover of both the landscape and the population of the island of Lolland: a radical transformation from the present-day reality of a depopulating and socially challenged province into an exclusive gated community for wealthy people with a mountain built on the rubbles of demolished social housing estates. Kaspar Colling Nielsen's novels have been translated and sold to a number of countries, and he has been compared to the French writer Michel Houellebecq. In 2019, Colling Nielsen became speech writer for the Danish Minister of Climate, while still operating as an author.

'Wilhelm and Jack were walking on Onsebjerg just outside Nakskov. Jack was still depressed but Wilhelm had managed to lure him out for a brisk morning walk.

"It's good that you're getting out a bit, Jack. You can't lie at home and rot."

"It doesn't matter. I can be here or there. It makes no difference."

Wilhelm flew up on his back and looked up towards the top of the mountain, which was covered by snow.

"This mountain was built from all the building materials from all the social housing they demolished on Lolland back in the day," said Wilhelm.

"What do you mean?"

"Well, before Lolland became the Lolland we know today, the island was the poorest place in Denmark."

No, I don't believe it."

"I'm not kidding. One of the reasons Onsebjerg was built was that they wanted to demolish all the ugly buildings where all the poor people lived and

build new expensive, exclusive ones so that the poor people couldn't afford to be here anymore. Onsebjerg is a monument to exclusion."

"I didn't know that. I thought the mountain had always been here."

"No, no, they built it. They built the entire shit, also the Maribo Hills."

"The Maribo Hills? That must have been a huge undertaking. They stretch all the way down to Nysted."

"Yes, that says something about how much social housing there was. The forest we're walking in was also planned and planted. Mount Copenhagen is still much bigger, even if you include the Maribo Hills. And, by the way, Onsebjerg is landscaped by the same person behind Mount Copenhagen back in the day. His name is Mik Thobo-Carlsen."

Wilhelm gave Jack a secretive look. The two friends walked in silence for some time. Jack stopped and looked out over the landscape. They were at 600 metres and below them there was nothing but forest and hills as far as the eye could see. The morning haze hung like a film over everything. On the meadow outside Nakskov there were grazing European bison. Jack inhaled the fresh morning air.'

(Excerpt from *The European Spring*, original title *Det Europæiske Forår*, by Kaspar Colling Nielsen, Gyldendal, 2017, translated by William Frost. excerpt published courtesy of the author's representative, Salomonsson Agency)

Colophon

THE WELFARE CITY IN TRANSITION

COPYRIGHT:
Copenhagen Architecture Festival
The Danish Architectural Press

EDITED BY:
Signe Sophie Bøggild
Pernille Maria Bärnheim
and Kristoffer Lindhardt Weiss

GRAPHIC DESIGN:
Alexis Mark

TRANSLATION:
Pernille Maria Bärnheim, Kristoffer Lindhardt Weiss and
Signe Sophie Bøggild, unless otherwise stated

PROOFREADING:
Cornelius Colding

EDITORIAL ASSISTANT:
Anne Sofie Lyngby

COVER PHOTO:
Aysha Amin

We wish to thank the KADK Library for generously
providing the majority of the visual archival material,
and all the authors of the texts we have quoted in the book

PRINT:
Narayana Press

PUBLISHED BY:
The Danish Architectural Press

1ST EDITION
Printed in Denmark, 2020
ISBN 978-87-7407-000-9

PUBLISHED WITH SUPPORT FROM:
Dreyers Fond
Realdania
and the City of Copenhagen

This book is published on the occasion of the 7th edition of Copenhagen Architecture Festival, entitled 'The Welfare City in Transition'. Initiated by Festival Director Josephine Michau.